W9-AWP-167

THE DESIGN & DRAFTING of PRINTED CIRCUITS

THE DESIGN & DRAFTING of PRINTED CIRCUITS

by Darryl Lindsey

founder of the renowned MASTERS P.C. DESIGN SCHOOL

Published by

The Innovators
Bishop Graphics, Inc.
Westlake Village, California 91359

The Innovators
Bishop Graphics, Inc.
® 5388 Sterling Center Drive
P.O. Box 5007
Westlake Village, California 91359

Printed in the United States of America

First printing, December 1978

Second printing, March 1979

Third printing, February 1980

Fourth printing, September 1980

Reorder No. 10000

ISBN 0-9601748-0-X

Library of Congress Catalog Card No. 79-57181

PREFACE

The *Use*, The *How* and The *WHY* of Printed Circuit Design are explained in this book. As a teaching tool, the book makes the reader think through problems by effectively explaining guiding principles, defining terms and outlining design and manufacturing processes.

Discussion of theories is in the light of the best commercial practices, making the book an accurate source of valuable information for the student as well as the industry practitioner.

The author discusses and weighs theories of design and their application in the commercial electronic field so that the book will serve as an organized technical aid. Clear and carefully selected illustrations will appeal to the many persons in industry who have had little opportunity to study P.C. Design.

The chapter on "Logic", provides a source of information that is difficult to find elsewhere. The understanding of logic as it relates to the P.C. Design greatly increases the value of the book as a text and as an important source of information.

The author's past experience and current state-of-the-art materials are presented in a manner calculated to help in the solution of future problems. To readers of this first edition it is the author's wish that this book will prove to be of lasting value.

ACKNOW-LEDGMENT

The author would like to express his thanks for all the assistance that has been provided for the various editions of this book. I am much indebted to former students, colleagues and friends for their time and efforts in helping prepare this book. I am indebted especially to the following: Don Coulthart, Gary Wilson and Don Sefervoich.

And finally to my wife, Priscilla Lindsey for her time and patience in helping me prepare the manuscript.

INTRODUCTION

Evolution of the printed circuit board does not "just happen". In fact, some rather serious thought must be given to each individual project before actual design work can begins. Once started, the design should proceed through six crucial phases. These phases are outlined in this introduction and are explained in detail within the corresponding section of this book.

Pre-design effort will ensure that the printed circuit board designer has a general knowledge of the project ahead of him, electrically and physically. Most of all, it will ensure that his ideas and those of the circuit design engineer coincide. Coordination between the circuit design engineer and the PCB designer *cannot* be overstressed. This communication link is of the utmost importance if the end product is going to meet *all* fit, form, and function requirements set forth.

Before work of any kind can be started, however, the circuit design engineer must prepare an appropriate "engineering" schematic. The engineering schematic is transferred to the PCB designer, and phase I of her/his work begins at this point. All too often, the schematic phase is not approached "head-on" and the remaining design phases suffer accordingly. To insure that you get off on the right foot, put that engineering schematic at the *top* of your "list of tools".

Printed circuitry and the printed circuit board, what are they? For years, printed circuitry and printed circuit boards have been defined and re-defined within the electronics industry. The following are definitions that have been extracted from leading electronics dictionaries:

> "A circuit in which the interconnecting wires have been replaced by conducting strips printed, etched, etc. onto an insulating board. It may also include similarly formed components on the base board."

> "Also called a card, chassis or plate. An insulating board onto which a circuit has been printed."

Of course, these definitions assume that the reader has had prior experience with point-to-point wire soldering. For those unfamiliar with the process, it simply required hand-soldering insulated wires between component leads where electrical connection was required. Simple it was. However, it was also time consuming and the end product was complicated, bulky, and truly a production nightmare. Understandably, compactness, efficiency in assembly, and standardization have since become the goal of electronic industries in the United States and abroad.

In contrast to modern electronic components used today, the "printed wiring board" (as it was formerly known) included designs with bulky, high-heat producing components such as vacuum tubes, large oil-filled capacitors and transformers. Miniaturization and micro-miniaturization seen in today's electronic components (such as diodes, transistors, integrated circuits, capacitors, resistors, and transformers) have played a leading role in speeding up and developing the techniques and standards employed in the production of today's printed circuit boards. This book is dedicated to *these* techniques and standards.

The author prefers to define the modern-day printed circuit board as follows:

"The replacement of hand-soldered, point-to-point wire connections with thin lines of copper. These copper lines are affixed on one or both sides of flat, rigid, glass-epoxy insulating boards through various processes including photography and chemical etching. The board facilitates the rapid assembly of active, passive, discrete, non-discrete, and hybrid electronic components with the following result: A single compact assembly where ease of assembly, maintenance and reliability are an order of magnitude better than ever before possible."

TABLE OF CONTENTS

Chapter

1

SCHEMATICS

Understanding schematics is an essential part, and should be considered primary, in the PCB design process. These schematics are written in a language foreign to the beginner, and are sometimes confusing to the experienced PCB designer. An attempt by the beginner to read a schematic would undoubtedly end up with chaotic results. Therefore, the PCB design process must be accomplished with a complete understanding of the schematic language.

Generation of the schematic is an interactive process that starts during the conceptual design phase and continues until the design is completed. Table 1-1 lists the steps that occur during the schematic development cycle. A typical sketch and the resulting schematic are shown in Figure 1-1.

The schematic diagram is composed of symbols that represent electrical and electromechanical components plus lines that represent conductors which interconnect components. The components are assigned reference designations to differentiate between similar symbols. The schematic of Figure 1-2 shows connecting lines, symbols and reference designations.

What Happens During the DESIGN CONCEPT PHASE	What Happens During the SCHEMATIC REDRAW PHASE
A. Rough schematic sketch by design engineer.	A. Clean-up and redraw by draftsman or printed circuit board designer.
B. P.C. Board in a breadboard design phase.	B. P. C. Board final design.
1. Used by engineer to layout breadboard of circuit(s) under development.	1. Purpose for this phase: Clean up schematic, standardize on symbols, develop good flow patterns, assign connector pin numbers, condense multiple sheets into a useable document.
2. Usually lacks; neatness, connector pins, and final components to be used.	2. A clean schematic will assure that the PCB design phase is more successful.
3. Usually is *not* under charge control, therefore must not be used by test department or by field service department.	3. Allows the PCB designer to get an idea of the components needed while removing unnecessary or component overage that were included in the breadboard phase.
4. Sometimes the circuit drawings are contained on many sheets of paper during the design phase. Try to visualize understanding a circuit under this constraint.	4. Release documentation package, with schematic, to Test, Publications, Field Service Dept. for their respective uses.
5. It's typically used for layout of the Printed Circuit Board.	

TABLE 1-1
Schematic Development Cycle

THIS SKETCH:

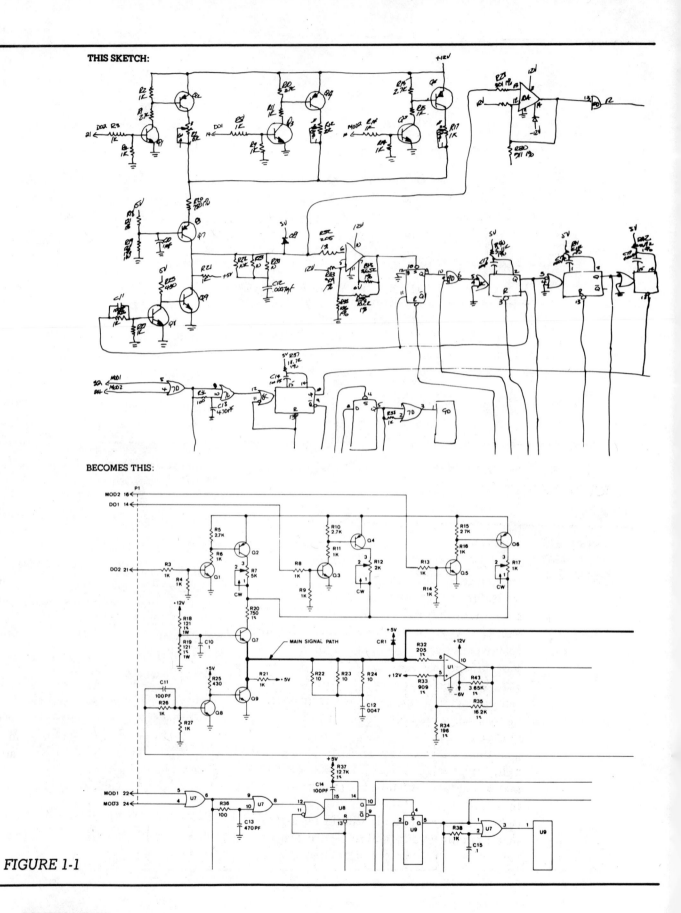

BECOMES THIS:

FIGURE 1-1

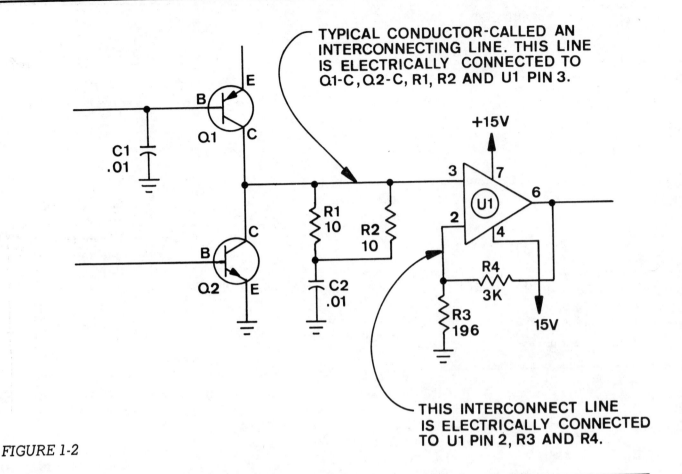

TYPICAL CONDUCTOR-CALLED AN INTERCONNECTING LINE. THIS LINE IS ELECTRICALLY CONNECTED TO Q1-C, Q2-C, R1, R2 AND U1 PIN 3.

THIS INTERCONNECT LINE IS ELECTRICALLY CONNECTED TO U1 PIN 2, R3 AND R4.

FIGURE 1-2

ABBREVIATIONS AND SYMBOLS

Reference designations are combinations of letters and numbers used to identify the components. The letters identify the type of electrical symbol and component such as: (Resistor $\mathord{-\!\!\wedge\!\!\wedge\!\!\wedge\!-}$ = R) and (Capacitor $\dashv\!\!\vdash$ = C). The number identifies the differences between electrical components of the same type: R1, R2, R3, C1, C2, C3, etc. All schematics using standard commercial practices should be drawn from *left* to *right*, input on the left side of the sheet and output on the right side. All reference designations will be numbered from left to right and top to bottom. In general, schematic diagrams should be arranged so that they can be read functionally from left to right. The overall result should be a schematic circuit layout (and reference designations) which follows the signal or transmission path from input to output.

Component Definitions.

Graphic symbols for electrical components are a form of shorthand and used to show the functioning of a part of a circuit. Many companies have standards of their own that are usually based on a combination of military and commercial source, Military MIL- STD-15, Industry ASA and American Standards Association Y14.5. It would be impractical to include all of the military and industry standards. Only the most commonly used symbols in schematics for printed circuit boards are described below.

CAPACITOR

Reference Designation: **C** Electronic Symbol: $\dashv\!\vdash$ or $\dashv\!\!\vdash$ A device consisting of two conducting surfaces separated by an insulating material or dielectric

ABBREVIATION	ITEM SYMBOL	ABBREVIATION	ITEM SYMBOL
AR	Amplifier	M	Gage or Meter
AT	Attenuator	MK	Transmitter, Microphone
B	Blower, Fan	MT	Transducer
BT	Battery	P	Connector Plug
C	Capacitor	PS	Power Supply
CB	Circuit Breaker	Q	Transistor
CP	Connector Adapter	R	Resistor—Variable or Fixed
CR	Diode	S	Switch
DC	Directional Coupler	T	Transformer
DS	Indicator—Lamp or Light	TB	Terminal Board
E	Terminal Post	TP	Test Point
F	Fuse	U	Integrated Circuit (IC)
FL	Filter	V	Vacuum Tube
G	Generator	VR	Voltage Rectifier
J	Jack-Connector Receptacle	W	Busbar or Cable
K	Relay	X	Socket, Fuse Holder or
L	Inductor or Coil		Lampholder
LS	Loudspeaker	Y	Crystal

TABLE 1-2
Abbreviations for
Reference
Designations

such as air, paper, mica, glass, plastic, film or oil. A capacitor stores electrical energy, blocks the flow of direct current, and permits the flow of alternating current, to a degree, dependent upon the capacitance and the frequency.

a. ⊣⊢
b. C1
c. .1uf
d. 25V
e. ±10%

Electronic Symbol: (See Item a)
Reference Designation: C (See Item b)
Value Expressed In: Farads (f) - most general applications (especially in P.C. boards) are in microfarads (uf) or pico farads (pf).

Tolerance: The tolerance reflects the amount that the capacitor is allowed to deviate from the value shown on the schematic. Most common tolerances for P.C. board applications are ±10% and ±20%.

Rating: Capacitors are rated by the amount of voltage that they are able to withstand safely. Capacitor physical sizes (of the same material) are controlled by their voltage ratings with most common values within a voltage rating all being the same size. Most common voltage ratings for P.C. board applications range from approximately 4 volts to several thousand volts.

Material: Capacitors used for P.C. Board mounting are most always constructed, externally, using metal, or paper. Internally, these capacitors use materials such as mica, foil, and mylar. There are various other methods of construction.

CONNECTOR PIN

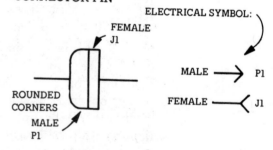

CRYSTAL

Reference Designation: **Y** *Electronic Symbol:* ⊣▯⊢ Generally employed to generate a signal with an accurate frequency output. Can also be used to convert pressure to an electrical signal, as can be done with piezo electric crystal transducer.

DIODE

Reference Designation: **CR** *Electronic Symbol:* ⊶ A two-terminal device which will conduct electricity more easily in one direction than in the other.

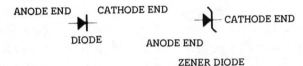

ANODE END   CATHODE END   CATHODE END

DIODE   ANODE END

ZENER DIODE

FUSE

Reference Designation: **F** *Electronic Symbol:* Two types of fuse symbols could be used. The top symbol represents the fuse element only. The bottom represents the complete fuse.

CHASSIS GROUND

Electronic Symbol: Indicates a connection made to the chassis.

COMMON GROUND

Electronic Symbol: Indicates a connection to ground.

INDUCTOR

Reference Designation: **L** *Electronic Symbol:* Used to introduce inductance into an electrical circuit. The inductor is wound into a spiral, or coil to increase its inductive intensity. It may employ an iron or air core.

RESISTOR

Reference Designation: **R** *Electronic Symbol:* A device which resists the flow of electric current in a circuit. There are two main types; fixed and variable.

     a.
     b. R1

c. 200 Ohms
d. ¼W
e. ±5%

Electronic Symbol: (See Item a)
Reference Designation: R (See Item b)
Value Expressed In: Ohms - (See Item c)
Tolerance: The tolerance reflects the amount that the resistor value is allowed to deviate from that shown on the schematic. Most common tolerances used in P.C. board applications are ±.1%, ±.5%, ±1%, ±2%, ±3%, ±5% and ±10%. (See item e)

Rating: Resistors are rated by the amount of wattage they are able to dissipate in a circuit. Resistor sizes (of the same material) are controlled by the wattage. The most common ratings for P.C. board applications are 1/10W, 1/8W, 1/4W, 1/2W and 1W (See Item d).

Material: Resistors are made from a variety of materials, but most commonly used on P.C. boards are carbon, wire-wound, and metal film.

RELAY

Reference Designation: **K** *Electronic Symbol:*

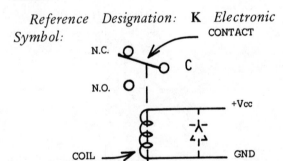

An electromechanical device with contacts that are opened and closed by a magnetic field, derived from a permanent magnet or electromagnet.

Rating: Relays are rated by (a) the amount of current that the contacts are designed to carry and i.e. (b) the voltage range at which the coil is designed to operate (i.e., 5V, 10V, 15V, and 100V).

NOTE: To protect the voltage source to the coil (especially in a transistor supply), a diode should be connected across the coil of the relay and physically located as near the coil as possible.

TRANSFORMER

Reference Designation: **T** *Electronic Symbol:*

An electrical device which, by electromagnetic induction, transforms electric energy from one or more circuits to one or more other circuits.

TRANSISTOR

Reference Designation: **Q** *Electronic*

Symbol:

A semiconductor device usually made of silicon or germanium having three or more electrodes. It may be used as an amplifier, signal generator, or to perform logical functions.

P-N-P Transistor
(Positive-Negative-Positive)

EMITTER COLLECTOR

BASE

N-P-N Transistor
(Negative-Positive-Negative)

EMITTER COLLECTOR

BASE

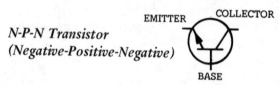

OPTIONAL
SOURCE OR SOURCE OR
DRAIN DRAIN

FET
(Field Effect Transistor)

GATE

VARIABLE RESISTOR

Reference Designation: **R** *Electronic Symbol:*

ZENER DIODE

Reference Designation: **VR** *Electronic Symbol:* A device that above a certain reverse voltage (the Zener value) has a sudden rise in current. If forward-biased, the diode is an ordinary rectifier.

The orientation of a symbol on a schematic drawing does not change the meaning of the symbol or its electrical function. See Fig. 1-3.

CONDUCTOR LINES

Interconnecting lines that represent the conductors on a schematic do not change weight to show differences of electrical changes. For example: voltage lines, ground lines and signal lines. However, some companies show heavier lines to emphasize the main signal path of a circuit. (See Figure 1-1)

SCHEMATIC ORGANIZATION

To avoid schematic confusion, do not spread the circuits out. Most schematics are made up of separate groups of transistors, resistors, and capacitors, etc. These groups or circuits should be layed out on the schematic drawing physically close to each other within the same group or circuit. Try not to intermix groups or circuits.

One very important rule to remember is that electrical components do not have to be shown in their physical, or actual P.C. board layout configuration.

CONDUCTOR LINES

In complex schematics, the interconnecting or conducting lines can present interpretation problems. To help eliminate the problem of hard-to-read schematics, a coding method is used. Figure 1-4 depicts use of the ground symbol to show interconnections to a common point. Parallel interconnecting conductor lines might be coded in the example of Figure 1-5.

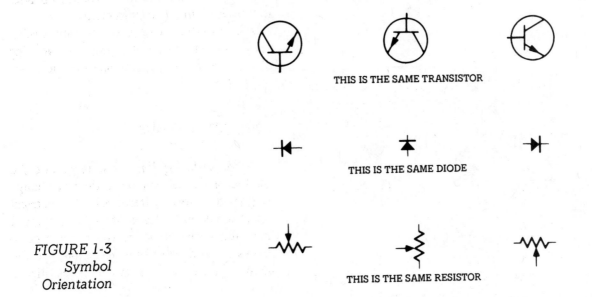

THIS IS THE SAME TRANSISTOR

THIS IS THE SAME DIODE

FIGURE 1-3
Symbol
Orientation

THIS IS THE SAME RESISTOR

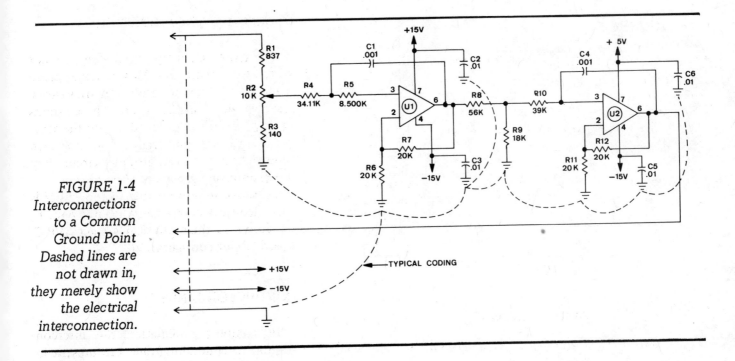

FIGURE 1-4
Interconnections
to a Common
Ground Point
Dashed lines are
not drawn in,
they merely show
the electrical
interconnection.

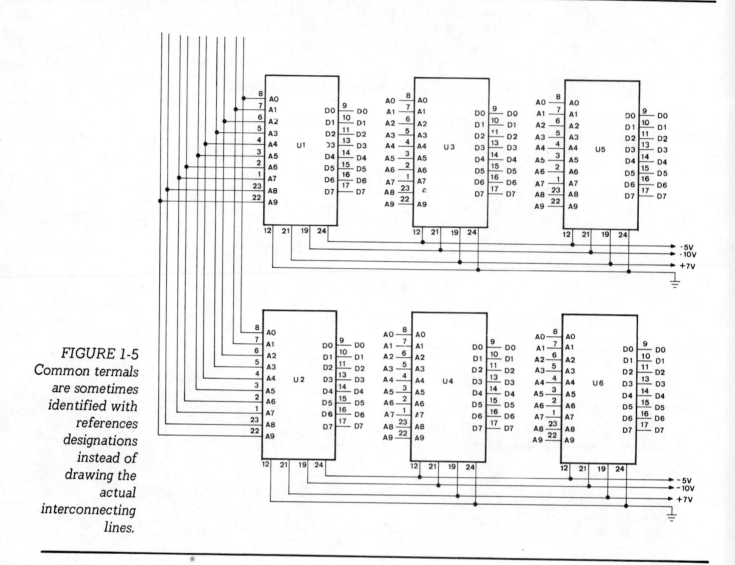

*FIGURE 1-5
Common termals
are sometimes
identified with
references
designations
instead of
drawing the
actual
interconnecting
lines.*

Chapter

2

BOARD LAYOUT GROUND RULES

The layout is undimensioned except for the board size and its relationship with mating structures and assemblies such as loading holes or special mounting fixtures. Tolerances should be included to facilitate further design and drafting.

Board layout and artwork should be made to the same scale whenever practical. After completion of the layout, an art-master (tape-up) is generated. The art-master is made to an enlarged scale (generally 2:1 or 4:1 depending on a particular company's standards). It is then photo-reduced by a photographer to provide a 1:1 scale negative and positive (master pattern) which becomes a highly accurate tool for the manufacturing of the P. C. Board.

Other documentation prepared from the layout and the reduced positive include fabrication plus assembly, parts list and silkscreen drawings, whatever special manufacturing sketches or aids that might be required. These are shown in Table 2-1.

Part numbers or other suitable identification such as component reference designations, test point designations, connector pin numbers, etc. taken from the schematic should be provided to identify all items and components appearing on the layout. The initial layout may start by arranging a rough sketch of the circuitry to determine the most practical placement of components and wiring (traces). The next step is to adopt the sketch to a formal layout using a grid and a component template which will establish very accurate conductor paths, component body outlines, component pad sizes, board outline, connector size and all other features. The layout should be drawn as viewed from the component side of the Printed Circuit Board. The grid pattern should be .050 or .100 inch spacing as shown in Figure 2-1.

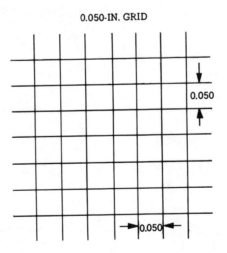

0.050-IN. GRID

0.050

0.050

FIGURE 2-1 Grid Layout Pattern for PCB's
FIGURE 2-2 Tape Spacing

1.0 Printed Circuit Documentation

Whether a PC board is to be a one-of-a-kind prototype, or a high-volume production article, it should have some informative type of documentation describing the means to the end. A printed-wiring drawing package should include the drawings shown below. Exactly *how much documentation,* and how it should be prepared will vary with budget and schedule as well as application.

Adequate documentation conveys to the user the basic electromechanical design concept, the type and quantity of parts and materials required, special manufacturing instructions, and up-to-date revisions.

Too little documentation results in misinterpretation, information gaps, and loss of uniform configuration. Manufacturing becomes dependent on individuals rather than documentation, often resulting in expensive rework and valuable lost time.

Too much documentation can result in increased drafting costs, and decreased manufacturing productivity due to

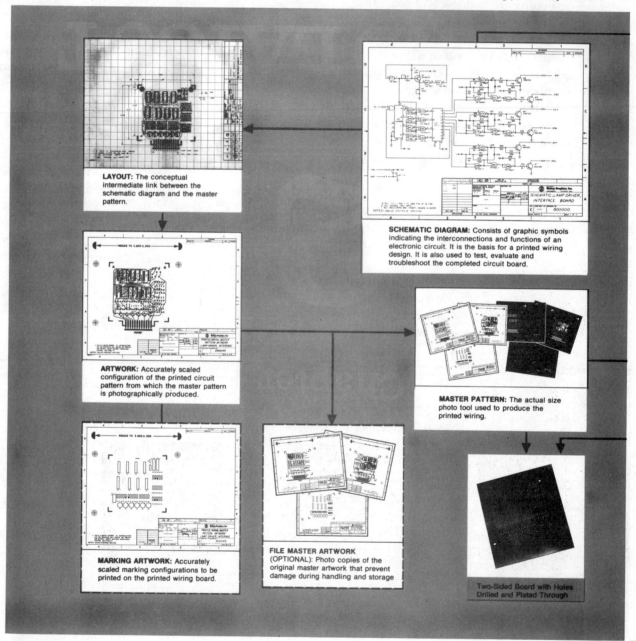

LAYOUT: The conceptual intermediate link between the schematic diagram and the master pattern.

SCHEMATIC DIAGRAM: Consists of graphic symbols indicating the interconnections and functions of an electronic circuit. It is the basis for a printed wiring design. It is also used to test, evaluate and troubleshoot the completed circuit board.

ARTWORK: Accurately scaled configuration of the printed circuit pattern from which the master pattern is photographically produced.

MASTER PATTERN: The actual size photo tool used to produce the printed wiring.

MARKING ARTWORK: Accurately scaled marking configurations to be printed on the printed wiring board.

FILE MASTER ARTWORK (OPTIONAL): Photo copies of the original master artwork that prevent damage during handling and storage

Two-Sided Board with Holes Drilled and Plated Through

TABLE 2-1

time-consuming interpretation of overly complicated and confusing drawings.

Printed wiring documentation may be divided into three classifications:

1. *Minimum—used for prototype and small quantity runs.*
2. *Formal—used for a standard product line and/or production quantities. Similar to Category E, Form 2 per MIL-D-1000 without source or specification support documentation.*
3. *Military—complies with government contracts specifying procurement drawings for the manufacture of identical items by other than the original manufacturer. (Category E, Form 1, per MIL-D-1000.)*

Standard format and reprographic drafting techniques are used extensively to reduce costs and improve drawing readability.

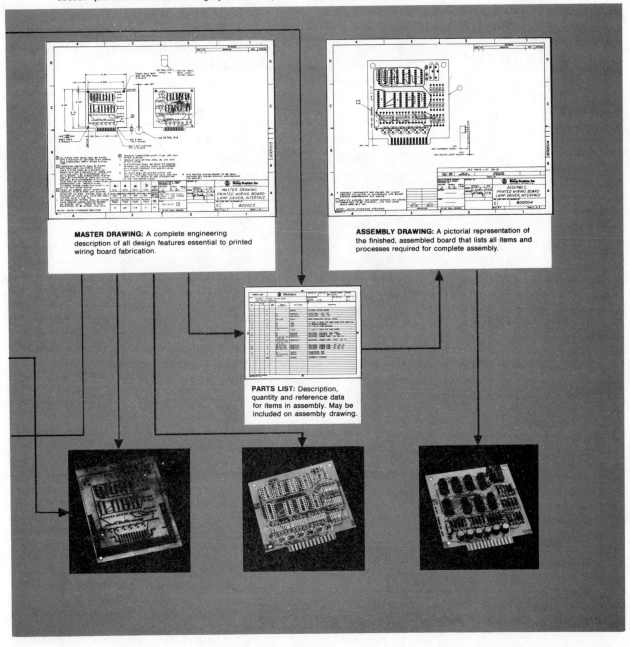

MASTER DRAWING: A complete engineering description of all design features essential to printed wiring board fabrication.

ASSEMBLY DRAWING: A pictorial representation of the finished, assembled board that lists all items and processes required for complete assembly.

PARTS LIST: Description, quantity and reference data for items in assembly. May be included on assembly drawing.

The board layout should be made to an enlarged scale. Either 2/1 or 4/1. All component pads should be located on grid intersections. The pad spacing for components should be determined by the maximum component body size. See standard formula in Chapter 4. All components should be mounted on only one side of the board. Components should be placed or located so that any component may be removed without removing any other component unless the assembly is not intended to be repaired.

Only one component lead should be placed in a lead hole except for some commercial bus bars that are designed to fit in the same mounting as the integrated circuit lead. When a board design requires that jumpers are to be used, (a jumper is a insulated wire used to substitute a trace on the board) they should be placed on the component side of the board and constructed of solid insulated wire designed to be as straight and as short as possible. Whenever possible avoid crossing over components. Components requiring special hold-downs because of shock, vibration or weight considerations should be so indicated on the layout. The type of fastening should also be specified; i.e., clamping, bolting, rat-tails, adhesive, etc.

CONDUCTOR WIDTH

The preferred board layout is done at 2/1 scale; therefore, it is logical that all traces, pads, air gap, etc. have to be multiplied by a factor of 2. For conductor width, establish a nominal size that suits the majority of applications.

SIGNAL TRACES

A signal trace is generally considered to be any trace on a board other than power and ground. These traces are generally low voltage and low current and, therefore they do not require a massive trace or air gap for proper function.

Traces on the PCB are produced by special adhesive tape that is applied to the layout during the design process. The most commonly accepted tape width used in industry today is .030-.040 in. at 2:1 scale with .030-.040 in. air gap between adjacent traces or pads. In cases of extremely dense boards, it is not uncommon to see tape-ups with .031- and even sometimes .026- in. wide traces; but it should be kept in mind that as the trace and air gap decrease, the cost and unreliability of the board increases. The .040-in. trace and air gap combination mentioned above provide a .020-in. conductor on the actual board. This combination provides ample material for conduction of electricity and also allows sufficient tolerance for the board manufacturing from the initial tape-up through the photography, etching, plating

TAPE WIDTH IN INCHES

.015	.050	.125	.187	.312	.800
.020	.062	.140	.200	.375	1.000
.026	.070	.150	.218	.400	2.000
.031	.080	.156	.250	.500	
.040	.093	.160	.280	.750	
.046	.100		.300		

TABLE 2-2

and wave soldering processes. Each of these steps should be allowed an acceptable amount of tolerance so that cumulative errors do not affect the reliability of the completed board.

In cases where the trace width (tape) must go down to .026- or .031-in. widths, it becomes very critical to try to maintain at least .040-in. air gap instead of an air gap the same width as the tape as illustrated in Fig. 2-2, the air gap should be adequate to avoid solder bridging between traces during the wave soldering operation.

POWER/ GROUND TRACES

The primary consideration in a power or ground trace is to provide a direct connection from the device to the power supply. Because this is not always possible, the next best step is to increase the width of the conductor trace so as to provide enough mass to accomplish essentially the same thing.

As shown in Fig. 2-3 a nominal trace width for power and ground can be established at .100-in. (2:1 scale). As in the case of the signal trace, this can be reduced for some requirements, but be sure the electrical engineer is aware of this condition. A .100-in. trace is also easy to plan as the design progresses due to the fact it is an even grid width and the air gap could be the same.

Color coding can be used in three different methods to provide helpful aids to the P.C. designer; i.e., conductor layer coding, voltage/ground pads, and input/output pads. Although each color coding method serves a separate distinct purpose, they are all used during the course of a typical P.C. layout.

A standard colored pencil such as those available from office supply or drafting supply outlets can be used for each color. Pick a readily available color to represent a particular voltage, ground or trace. Become familiar with what it represents and do not change. This avoids the confusion of what each color means on each board. After using these approaches for awhile, you will automatically relate the color code to its function without referring to a color key. (Color code pads only)

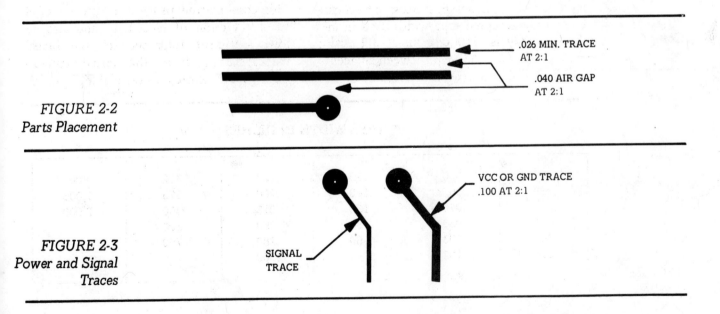

FIGURE 2-2
Parts Placement

.026 MIN. TRACE
AT 2:1

.040 AIR GAP
AT 2:1

FIGURE 2-3
Power and Signal Traces

VCC OR GND TRACE
.100 AT 2:1

SIGNAL TRACE

CONDUCTOR LAYER CODING

This coding system indicates which side of the PCB a particular trace is located. Therefore, on a typical two-sided board, two different colors would be used; i.e., red traces indicate component side traces, blue traces indicate non-component side traces. The component body outlines would be drawn with yet another color such as blue or some color that you would not plan to use for any of the other color coding methods. If a board is intended to be single-sided (all conductors on one side of the board only), then all traces should be one color only. This is shown in Figure 2-4. See Chapter 7, Figure 7-9

VOLTAGES/GROUND CODING

In this method, a different color is chosen to represent each voltage and ground that is used; i.e., red might be +5V,

orange +12V, green -12V, and blue ground. This is accomplished by color coding the component lead pad that is to be connected to the particular voltage or ground. (Pad only)

During the design stage, the colors stand out as flags to indicate where the nearest voltage or ground point is located for the most direct hook-up. This keeps the traces very direct and in most analog boards, allows the designer to wait until the layout is near completion to hook all the respective traces together.

During the taping operation, the color coded pad on the layout can be seen through the hole in the pad on the artwork. As shown in Figure 2-5 a general rule would tell the PCB taper that all color coded pads were to be .100-in. tape minimum regardless of the color; all other traces could be .050-in. wide or whatever size you choose.

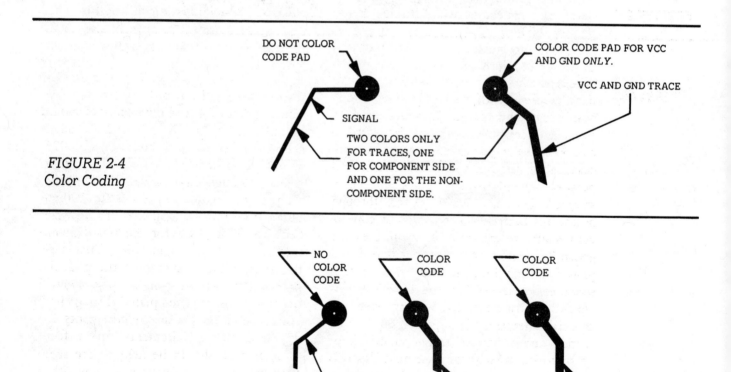

FIGURE 2-4
Color Coding

FIGURE 2-5

OUTPUT CODING

Terminals (pads) that are to be connected to a connector(s) may also use a color coding method. As the circuit is being laid out, the particular pad that is to go out to the connector can be color coded and left to be routed after the rest of the layout is completed. This allows the designer to complete the connections between local related components and then route the output connections (traces to the connector) in whatever path is most available and less crowded. The colors used for this purpose would be different from those used for voltage/ground coding and each different color would represent a particular connector; i.e., brown - J1, violet - J2.

TEMPLATES

A standard component template is one of the most necessary pieces of equipment the designer will use in P.C. design. It not only saves valuable time but also assures that standard component lead spacing and body sizes are considered. Although several models and styles are available, pick one that will be compact, yet complete for the requirements of your particular type of design. See FIG. 2-6

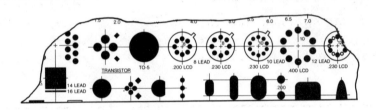

FIGURE 2-6

FEED THROUGHS

A feed-through consists of a pad on both sides of the board with a plated-through hole connecting them. They are used to connect traces on one side of the board to traces on the opposite side when a component pad is not available to accomplish this purpose. Feed-through holes are constructed like any other plated through holes; but because no terminals or component leads are mounted in them, they are generally smaller than any other pad and plated-through hole in order not to consume excess space on the board that is needed for trace routing. Feed-throughs are especially necessary in digital layouts where vertical and horizontal traces must be kept on opposite sides as much as possible. This method requires that a trace be routed in one direction as far as possible, then a feed-through pad located and the connection is continued on the opposite side of the board.

Feed-through sizes vary depending on the density of the board; but on tape-ups (where practical), feed through pads should be .125-in. This results in a .062-in. pad on the actual board which could have a .025- to .031-in. diameter hole drilled through it.

Feed-through pads smaller than .125-in. are used in many cases; i.e., .090-, .100-in., but a hole smaller than .025-in. diameter becomes impractical for the board manufacturer to drill in quantities. Therefore, the smaller the diameter of the pad, the narrower the annular ring (see page 37) will become on the finished plated-through pad.

In general, the pad size requirements and the hole size requirements for a feed-through hole should be held to the same standards and specifications of any other plated-through hole.

Chapter

3

DISCRETE COMPONENT LAYOUT

The following steps should be taken prior to laying out a PCB. These will simplify the design process.

1. All symbols or reference designations used by the engineer should be understood.

2. The specification sheet must be used to identify the case size or the body width and length (maximum size).

3. The case size should be used to determine the lead spacing to mount the component on the P.C. board (See following for minimum dimensions over maximum case size for lead spacing.) See Chapter 4, page 33

4. Polarity must be determined for all polarized components such as capacitors, diodes (must identify the cathode end) and some transistors (must identify the emitter, base and collector).

5. The lead diameter must be determined in order to select a pad size on our layout. See Chapter 4, page 37

6. Determine pad orientation looking from top view of components such as the transistor's emitter, base and collector, potentiometer or variable resistor Pins 1, 2 and 3, variable capacitors, relays, transformers, coils, etc.

7. Convert or establish component sizes at a 2/1 or 4/1 scale, which will be the same size of the layout. At this point, try to find most component sizes on the P.C. design template; for example, ¼W resistors (RL07 case size), ½W resistors, diodes, ceramic disc capacitors TO-5 and TO-18 case transistors, and many more depending on which template you use.

8. Before using the schematic to electrically group and connect components, look at the space requirements. This will conserve space relative to the different size components on a typical P.C. board. Figure 3-1 shows how important arrangement versus size can be.

POOR PLACEMENT   GOOD PLACEMENT

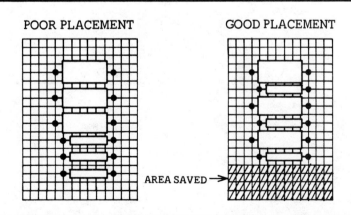

AREA SAVED →

FIGURE 3-1
Parts Placement

9. The schematic in Figure 3-2 will be used to illustrate the grouping of discrete components.

   a. Assuming steps 1 through 8 have been considered for component sizes, check to see that all components have the proper reference designators.

   b. The initial layout may start by arranging a rough arrangement of the components to determine the most practical placement. The component could be drawn in a rough form; use the template at this point, see example of Figure 3-3 using the schematic of Figure 3-2.

10. The "Correct Method" of Figure 3-3 is just one way to group the components in Figure 3-2: there are several ways that would be considered correct. One point it does show is that a component must be selected to work around or build from such as transistor Q1. In this case, the transistor is the key component because it connects to more components than any other one component on the schematic. Another point to consider is the shape of the grouped components. Try to group components in a square or rectangular shape. Refer to Figure 3-4 "Incorrect Method"; this shape is difficult to work with as far as adding circuits to the board at a later date or

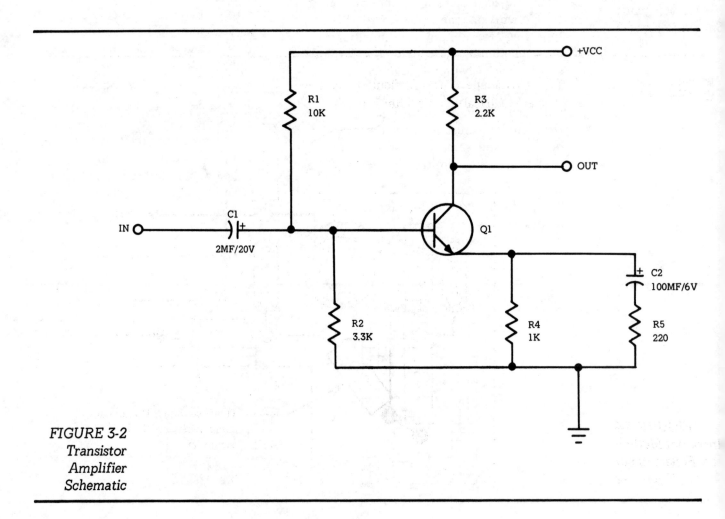

FIGURE 3-2
Transistor
Amplifier
Schematic

working additional components around this shape.

11. The layout of Figure 3-5 is electrically the same as Figure 3-4. With the same electrical connections, the components can be arranged differently.

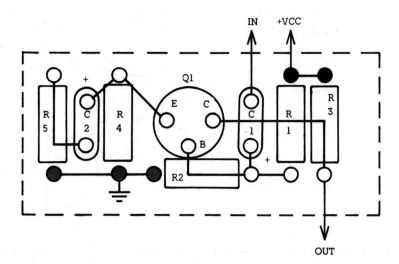

PADS = +VCC
PADS = GND
IN
+VCC
Q1
E
C
B
R 5
C 2
R 4
C 1
R 1
R 3
R2
OUT

FIGURE 3-3 Correct Layout for Schematic Shown in Fig. 3-2

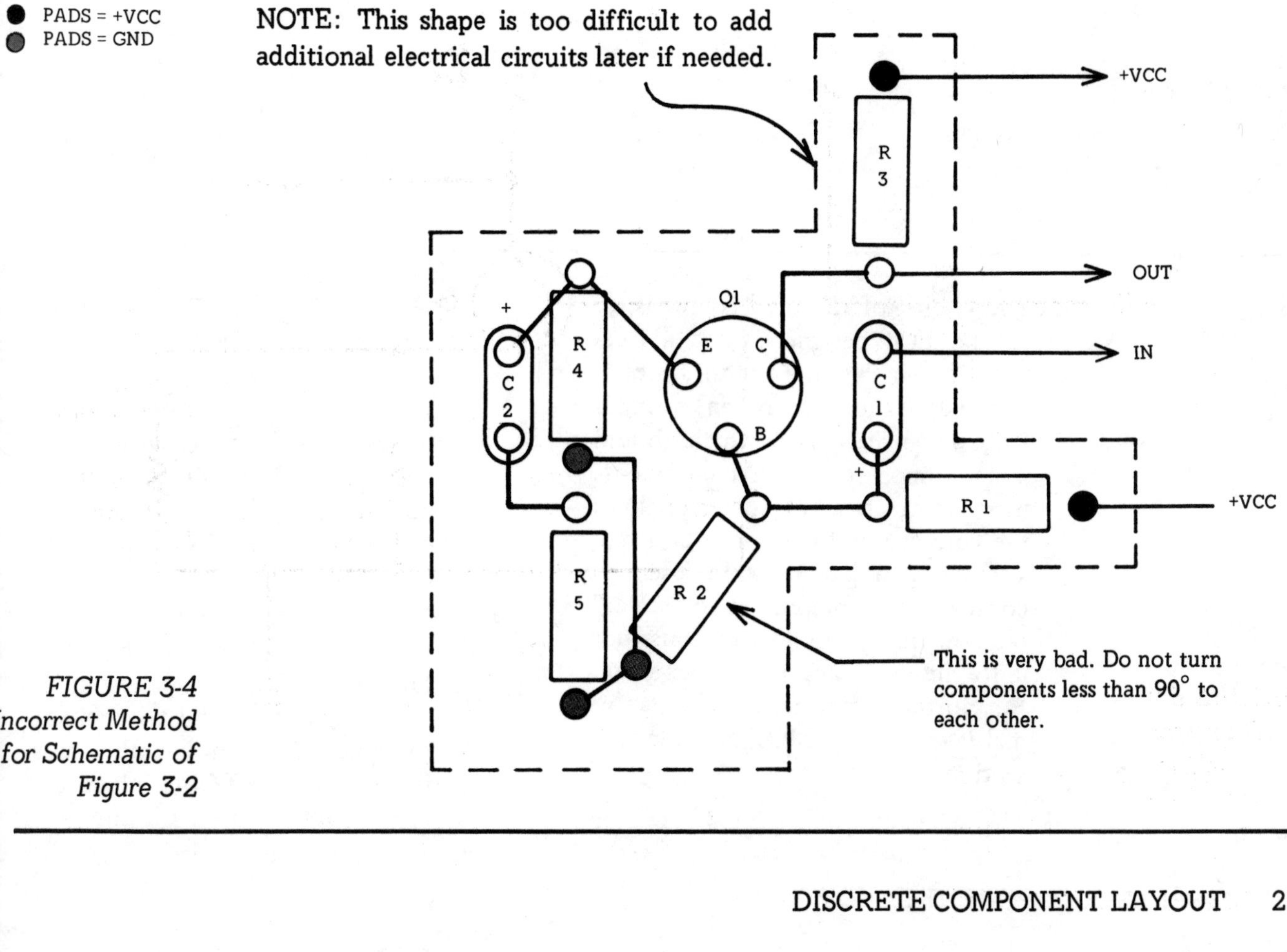

PADS = +VCC
PADS = GND
NOTE: This shape is too difficult to add additional electrical circuits later if needed.
+VCC
R 3
OUT
IN
Q1
E
C
B
C 2
R 4
C 1
R 1
+VCC
R 5
R 2
This is very bad. Do not turn components less than 90° to each other.

FIGURE 3-4 Incorrect Method for Schematic of Figure 3-2

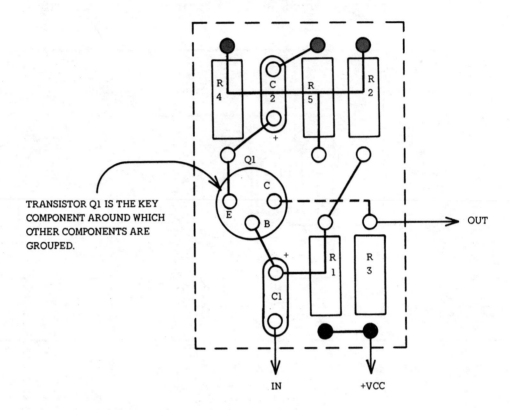

- PADS = +VCC
- PADS = GND

TRANSISTOR Q1 IS THE KEY
COMPONENT AROUND WHICH
OTHER COMPONENTS ARE
GROUPED.

FIGURE 3-5
Another Layout
for Schematic of
Figure 3-2

12. The choice of the final layout is up to the PCB designer. Once a free-hand rough layout (not to scale) is selected, it must be redone using a P.C. design template which should include most common components used. If the template does not have the correct size for the components, a circle template must be used to construct the component to "scale." Be sure that you select or construct it to the maximum component size. For further information about formal layout, see the P.C. board layout section.

13. The schematic of Figure 3-6 will be used as a second grouping exercise of discrete components.

a. Assuming Steps 1 through 8 in the beginning of this chapter have been considered for the component sizes, check to see that all components have the proper reference designators.

b. Again as in Step 9b, the initial layout should start by arranging a rough layout of the components to quickly determine the most practical and effective placement electrically and mechanically.

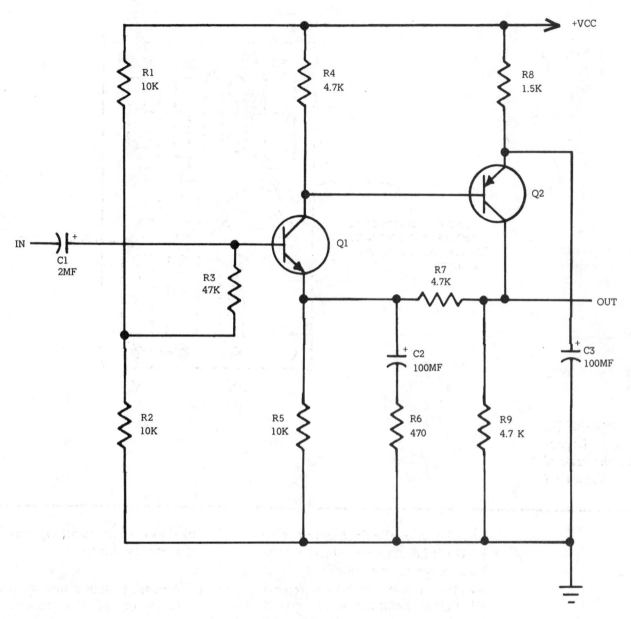

*FIGURE 3-6 Two
Transistor
Amplifier
Schematic*

14. Figure 3-7 is a rough layout of the Correct Method for the Schematic Figure 3-6.

15. The layout of Figure 3-8 shows the wrong way to spread out components. By *not* grouping in a square or rectangular shape, you *wasted* area.

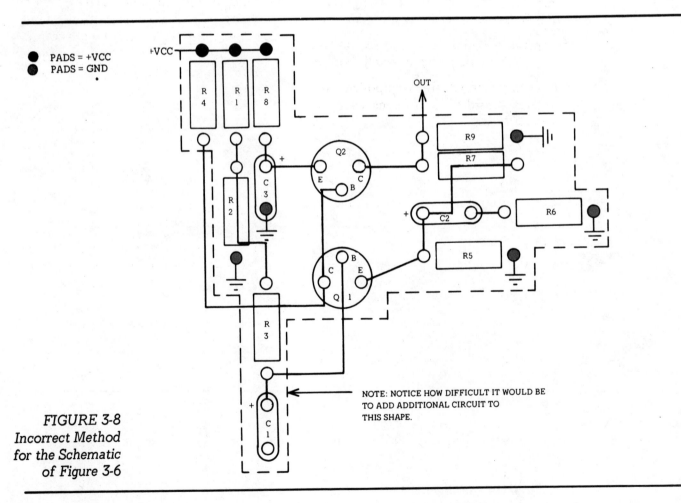

FIGURE 3-7
"Correct
Method" for the
Schematic of
Figure 3-6

● PADS = +VCC
● PADS = GND

+VCC

OUT

Q2

E   C

B

C3

R1

R8

R7

R9

C2

+

Q1

B

C

E

R2

R4

R3

R5

R6

+

C1

IN

FIGURE 3-8
Incorrect Method
for the Schematic
of Figure 3-6

● PADS = +VCC
● PADS = GND

+VCC

OUT

R4

R1

R8

R2

C3

Q2

E   C

B

R9

R7

C2

+

R6

C

B

E

Q 1

R5

R3

+

C1

NOTE: NOTICE HOW DIFFICULT IT WOULD BE
TO ADD ADDITIONAL CIRCUIT TO
THIS SHAPE.

PROBLEM AREAS OF ANALOG— P.C. BOARDS (DISCRETE COMPONENT LAYOUT)

1. Predetermine location of all components which are dictated by special structural considerations.

2. Arrange components so as to achieve the optimum shape for the P.C. board.

3. Some components should have short traces or interconnects (engineer will advise).

4. Some components should not be placed near each other to prevent magnetic or capacitive coupling (engineer will advise).

5. High potential differences between certain conductors will make it necessary to increase the space between such conductors.

6. Metal case (without insulator) components should not touch each other. Case could be electrically hot.

7. Separate grounds could be used on the same schematic. (Engineer will advise.)

8. Placement of variable components on the P.C. board should be considered for ease of access.

9. Size of voltage and ground traces.

10. Signal traces should be considered in the layout before voltage or ground traces. (Typically the voltage or ground traces can be as long as you wish).

11. Ground planes are very common on analog P.C. boards and should be considered in the initial layout. Some components use ground patterns for electrostatic shielding.

12. Some components require heat sinks (very common with transistors). (Engineer will advise).

13. Locate heat-sensitive and heat-radiating components as far apart as practical. But try not to locate the heat-radiating components together.

14. Components weighing ½ oz or more should not be supported by the leads solder joint alone, but should be provided with additional means of support such as brackets or clamps.

Chapter

4

MOUNTING COMPONENTS

Component mounting is probably the most important step in the printed circuit board design phase. The importance is simply that a specific number of components must be mounted onto a P.C. board with specific dimensions. This is complicated by some pretty rigorous spacing standards which make the job of mounting a seemingly difficult one. However, by following some basic rules, the job can be made fairly uncomplicated.

One of the most important steps the designer must perform is to determine how an actual component will be mounted into a finished P.C. board. Try to imagine an assembler trying to stuff resistors with .025-in. diameter leads into .020-in. pad holes. The consequences are dreary. Follow the steps below and this should never happen. Figure 4-1 shows the details of component mounting.

The three steps in component mounting are to determine pad spacing, P.C. board hole (drill) diameter, and pad diameter.

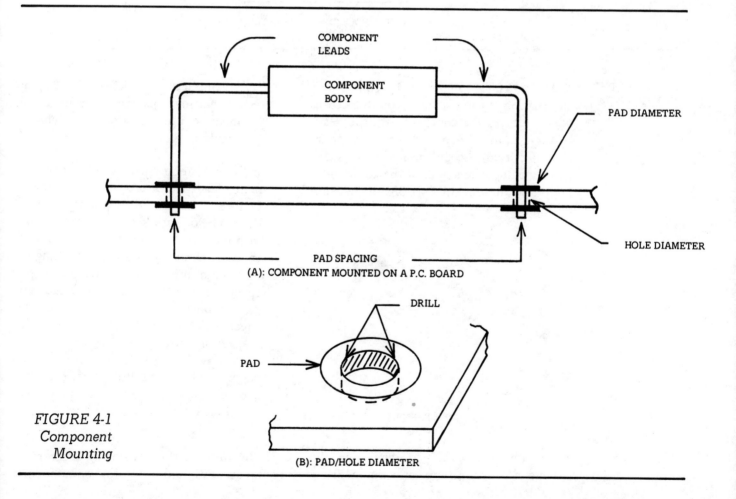

FIGURE 4-1
Component
Mounting

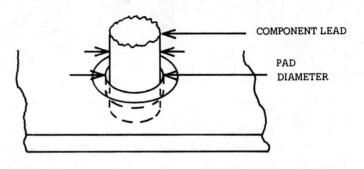

COMPONENT LEAD

PAD DIAMETER

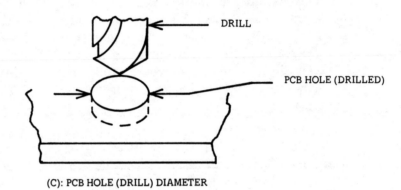

DRILL

PCB HOLE (DRILLED)

(C): PCB HOLE (DRILL) DIAMETER

FIGURE 4-1
Component Mounting

DETER-MINING PAD SPACING

As shown in Figure 4-1, component pad spacing is the distance from the center of one lead to the center of the other lead. (Although more than two leads are possible, only two are shown here). This distance includes the length of the component body plus the unbent portions of the component leads.

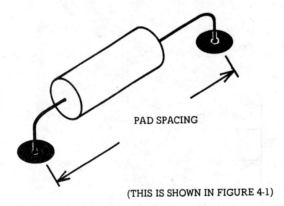

PAD SPACING

(THIS IS SHOWN IN FIGURE 4-1)

There are three ways to determine the spacing of pads for a typical component:

1. The manufacturer will provide the correct mounting (spacing) information in the manufacturer's catalog, in which case no calculations are necessary.

2. If the mounting (spacing) of the component's leads is not provided in the manufacturer's catalog, then check to see if the body or case size is given. In most manufacturer's catalogs, the maximum case size dimensions are listed. Using the maximum dimensions, the correct pad spacing can be determined. This is a typical commercial manufacturer's spec sheet which would be found in a catalog (capacitor catalog). The size can be found by looking up the voltage and value of the capacitor. The capacitor shown is just an example of one type of radial lead component. See Fig. 4-4, 4-2.

3. The third method is not as accurate as methods 1 and 2. If the component's

mounting or hole spacing cannot be found from the manufacturer's catalog or the case size (for axial or radial components), the actual part must be scaled. Try to pick up a sample from the manufacturer or distributor. Once the part is obtained, then use the same formula as in method 2 and determine the pad spacing by scaling the part to get the maximum body length required on an axial lead component or just the distance between the leads for a radial lead component.

HOLE DIAMETER & PAD SIZE

Hole diameter and pad size depend on each other. Using the formula listed below, the hole size must be determined before a pad size is selected. To calculate the hole diameter, the maximum lead diameter of the component to be inserted must be known.

Lead Diameter: Finding the lead diameter of a component can be done in two ways: First by looking in a manufacturer's catalog and finding the maximum diameter as listed; second by obtaining the actual part and scaling the lead diameter. The first choice is by far more accurate.

Hole Diameter Formula: .006-in. minimum to .020-in. maximum over the maximum lead diameter = the minimum hole size as shown in Figure 4-5.

Pad Spacing Formula: In order to use this formula, the case size of the component (axial lead type) must be known. Fig. 4-2.

Take the maximum body (case) size length "X" + .060-in. minimum on each side from body to centerline of each lead = pad spacing (This will give the minimum spacing between pads). An important point to keep in mind is that this formula gives the *minimum* spacing. Because most components are laid out on even tenth or .100-in. spacing at 2/1 scale, this is called or referred to as laying out on "grid."

Example: If calculations for the spacing of a component worked out to be ".460 thousands" at 2/1 scale, round this off to ".500" at 1/1 or "1.000" at 2/1 scale.

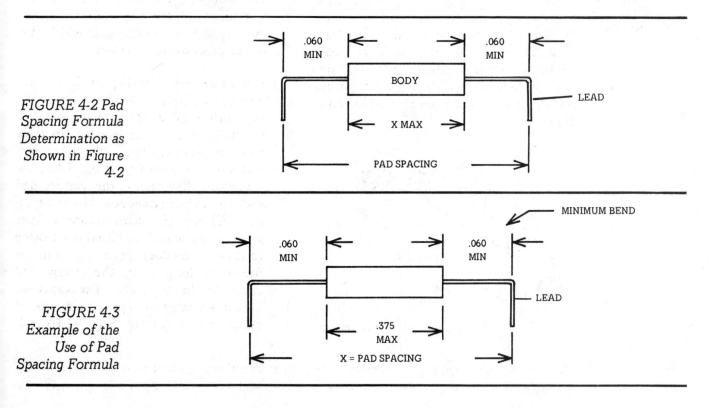

FIGURE 4-2 Pad Spacing Formula Determination as Shown in Figure 4-2

.060 MIN   .060 MIN   BODY   LEAD   X MAX   PAD SPACING

FIGURE 4-3 Example of the Use of Pad Spacing Formula

MINIMUM BEND   .060 MIN   .060 MIN   LEAD   .375 MAX   X = PAD SPACING

Working Exercise-See Figure 4-3

X = .375-in. maximum + .060-in. x 2 = pad spacing

.375	body length
.060	minimum bend
+.060	minimum bend
.495	minimum pad spacing

The .495 dimension would work, but to stay on grid, we would round this off to .500 at 1/1 or 1.000 at 2/1 scale.

NOTE: When rounding off axial lead type components, try to round off in these increments at 1/1 scale: .200, .250, .300, .400, .500, .600, .700, .800, .900, and 1.000.

Radial Lead Components: Radial lead components have no standard formula such as the axial lead components. Instead, you must rely on the manufacturer to supply you with the proper hole or pad spacing. See example in Figure 4-4.

Pad Size Formula: Minimum .020-in. annular ring over the maximum hole size (.020 annular ring is for reference only)

NOTE: Applying the formula of .020-in. minimum annular ring over the maximum lead diameter will give minimum size pad that could be used. This minimum size pad diameter may not be a standard size pad that can be bought. If this is so, simply round off to the next higher standard pad size.

Example: (Manufacturer's spec sheet tolerance .019″±.002 diameter). See Fig. 4-5 or Fig. 4-5A.

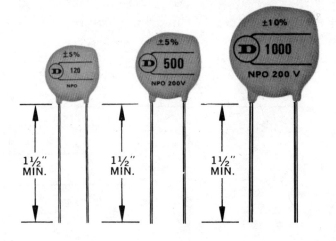

DIAMETER MAX.	CAPACITANCE RANGE		LEAD SPACING*
	200 VDC	500 VDC	
.225″	1-22 pf	1-18 pf	.187″
.285″	23-43	19-30	.250″
.345″	44-68	31-50	.250″
.385″	69-91	51-75	.250″
.440″	92-130	76-100	.250″
.520″	131-150	101-135	.375″
.575″	151-200	136-150	.375″
.675″	201-250	151-210	.375″
.735″	251-300	211-240	.375″
.770″	301-350	241-270	.375″
.850″	351-500	271-360	.375″

*ROUND OFF TO THE NEXT HIGHER GRID (.100 GRID)

FIGURE 4-4
Capacitor Mounting Data

TYPICAL AXIAL LEAD COMPONENT

Step 1—The manufacturer's spec sheet example above lists the lead diameter as .019-in. with a tolerance of ±.002″. Now add the tolerance ±.002 to the lead diameter .019:

.019   Lead diameter
+.002   Tolerance
.021   Maximum lead diameter

Step 2—Once the maximum lead diameter is established, add the minimum clearance which is .006-in. to the maximum lead diameter.

.021   Maximum lead diameter
+.006   Minimum clearance around lead
.027   Minimum hole size

Step 3—Once the minimum hole diameter is established, find the maximum hole diameter. The maximum clearance over the lead is .020-in.

.021   Maximum lead diameter
+.020   Maximum clearance over the lead
.041   Maximum hole diameter

Step 4—Two hole sizes (minimum and maximum) have been established. Use this to find which size hole would best fit as many other components as possible on the P.C. board layout (See example below).

Example: Compare the minimum and maximum hole diameters of component "A" to component "B" to see if a hole size can be selected that will fit both components Figure 4-5. This can be done by examining the range of hole sizes for components "A" and "B."

Component "A" holes sizes range from a minimum of .027- through .041-in.

Component "B" hole sizes range from a minimum of .034- through .048-in.

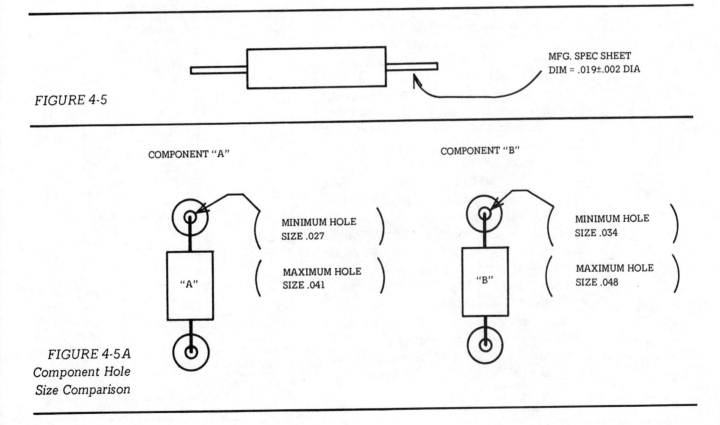

FIGURE 4-5

MFG. SPEC SHEET
DIM = .019±.002 DIA

COMPONENT "A"

MINIMUM HOLE SIZE .027

MAXIMUM HOLE SIZE .041

"A"

COMPONENT "B"

MINIMUM HOLE SIZE .034

MAXIMUM HOLE SIZE .048

"B"

FIGURE 4-5A
Component Hole Size Comparison

```
           Min.   .027
         Comp.   .028
          "A"    .029
                 .030
                 .031
                 .032
                 .033

           Min.   .034
         Comp.   .035
          "B"    .036
                 .037
                 .038
                 .039
                 .040

           Max.   .041
         Comp.   .042
          "A"    .043
                 .044
                 .045
                 .046
                 .047

           Max.   .048
         Comp.
          "B"
```

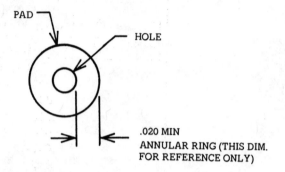

```
.037        HOLE DIAMETER (MAXIMUM)
+.040       .020 MINIMUM ANNULAR RING X 2
.077        MINIMUM SIZE PAD THAT COULD BE USED
```

To choose a size that will fit both component "A" and "B", select a size above the minimum of "A" and "B" but not to exceed the maximum of "A" and "B"; .037-in. or .038-in. could be used. To be exact, .035-in. through .040-in. diameters.

In conclusion of Step 4, the hole size for Figure 4-5 component would be between the minimum of .027-in. diameter and the maximum of .041-in. diameter depending upon the other components on our P.C. board such as the above.

Step 5—At this point, a hole size for the component or components could be established. Next a pad size for the P.C. board can be selected using the formula previously given in this chapter.

Pad Size Formula: .020-in. minimum annular ring over the maximum hole size. (.020 min. annular ring is for reference only) Use .037-in. diameter for hole size.

| OD | | ID | | CAT. |
in.	mm	in.	mm	NO.
.050	1,27	.015	0,38	D135
.062	1,57	SOLID		S101
		.025	0,63	D136
.075	1,90	SOLID		S121
.080	2,03	.031	0,79	D216
.088	2,23	SOLID		S119
.093	2.36	SOLID		S102
		.031	0,79	D137
		SOLID		S123
		.031	0,79	D101
.100	2,54	.040	1,02	D207
		.050	1,27	D211
		.062	1,57	D148
		SOLID		S103
		.025	0,63	D180
		.031	0,79	D102
.125	3,17	.040	1,02	D179
		.050	1,27	D230
		.062	1,57	D169
		.031	0,79	D144
		.040	1,02	D203
.150	3,81	.050	1,27	D164
		.062	1,57	D231
		.080	2,03	D165

TABLE 4-1

TYPICAL PAD SIZE SELECTION CHART

OD		ID		CAT. NO.
in.	mm	in.	mm	
.156	3,96	SOLID		S104
		.031	0,79	D103
.175	4,45	SOLID		S120
		SOLID		S122
		.025	0,63	D181
		.031	0,79	D138
.187	4,75	.040	1,02	D104
		.050	1,27	D150
		.062	1,57	D105
		.093	2,36	D182
		SOLID		S124
		.025	0,63	D183
		.031	0,79	D139
		.040	1,02	D204
.200	5,08	.050	1,27	D158
		.062 ▪	1,57	D147
		.062	1,57	D206
		.080	2,03	D106
		.093	2,36	D184
.208	5,28	.062	1,57	D168
		SOLID		S105
		.031	0,79	D140
.218	5,54	.040	1,02	D143
		.050	1,27	D155
		.062	1,57	D107

Step 6—The next step and last is to choose a pad that will fit or accommodate as many hole sizes as possible. Try not to select too many different sizes. Table 4-1 is a typical pad size selection chart.

Using the minimum size pad established in Step 5 (which is .077-in. diameter), convert all our diameters and pad diameters to the scale that the layout and tape-up are made (2:1 scale). Therefore, .077-in. x 2 = .154-in. diameter minimum. Now look at the pad size chart in Table 4-1 and select a pad size above .154-in. diameter.

NOTE: A good choice would be .187-in. diameter on the chart, but .156-in. through .350-in. could be used. The most important thing to remember is not to come too close to the minimum size that could be used, if possible.

A scale of 2/1 was used as the example of Step 6; a scale of 4/1 could have been used.

Chapter

5

LOGIC

The printed circuit board design process is evolutionary and consists of many phases. These phases may or may not be accomplished in a specific order. All however, will ultimately be required and accomplished through necessity. Digital logic is one of the evolutionary phases. Since you may not even know the meaning of the words "digital logic," it is the primary intent of this chapter to describe digital logic as an aid to the printed circuit board design process.

Component combining and grouping which are the real secrets to a successful PCB layout is a secondary intent of this chapter. Grouping will be discussed following the digital logic discussion. It is felt that an understanding of digital logic is a must before component grouping can be accomplished successfully.

This chapter will not make you an electronics technician nor will it make you an electronics engineer. Instead, you will have sufficient knowledge of digital logic to perform your P.C. board designing tasks more effectively and efficiently.

Experience has shown that understanding digital logic and applying this knowledge can solve many problems in the initial design stages rather than at the scheduled completion time. It is through problem solving that an understanding of digital logic is without a doubt an aid in the P.C. board design process.

The word "digital" is derived from the word digit which means number, such as the 1, 2, 3, 7, 9 digits. However, in the science of modern electronics certain words, or jargon have taken on a different meaning from those published by Webster. Also, certain other words are assumed to be included in many electronic definitions. For instance, the word digital not only means digits, but implies "binary," which means two-state (as opposed to decimal which means ten-state). Therefore, combining the apparent and not-so-apparent definition, the word digital, as you will know it, means: digits that can be in two states (two-state electronics). These two states are: 0, *Off* or Low and 1, *On,* or High.

Logic is the science of valid, efficient reasoning. In other words, it is a way of performing a given task in the most efficient manner available to you. As in the definition of digital, the word logic implies digital electronics. Combining the apparent and not-so-apparent, the words "digital logic" mean: An effective decision making, method using two-state electronics, is relatively inexpensive (as opposed to non-digital logic electronics), and is most useful in the art of electronic design. Digital integrated circuits or IC's, are the hardware through which the digital logic concept is made possible.

The IC is a relatively small, sealed package with pins protruding from the sides, ends, top, or bottom. The package types are; dual-in-line packages (DIP) (See Figure 5-1) flat pack, and T0-5 can. As the name implies, *circuits* NOT just *components* are integrated, built-into, the IC. There are three common families of Integrated Circuits available today. They are:

SSI - Small Scale Integration
MSI - Medium Scale Integration
LSI - Large Scale Integration

The difference between these three is not the types of circuits contained within each package, but the density of circuitry contained within. Each of these three families can be further subdivided into the type of circuitry used to fabricate the particular IC device. These subdivisions are:

TTL - Transistor transistor logic
ECL - Emitter coupled logic
CMOS - Complimentary metal oxide
       semiconductor logic
DTL - Diode transistor logic
RTL - Resistor-transistor logic
HTL - High-threshold logic

Our intention here is to point out some of the abbreviations used in the industry today, not to define each one in detail. The difference between these types are: switching speed, power consumption, cost, isolation, and sensitivity.

The word "circuit" warrants definition. A circuit, as opposed to a component, is made up of many discrete components such as resistors, capacitors, transistors, and diodes that can perform some function. For example, it might count up, count down, multiply or divide. In fact, it might do all at the same time. Whereas, the discrete component cannot perform a function readily without first being connected into a circuit.

Integrated circuits are usually formed on a silicon wafer consisting of a multitude of circuits. Various photographic and chemical etching processes are performed to produce the pre-designed electronic circuits. Then the individual circuits are separated from the wafer and are usually called die or chips. Gold wires are connected

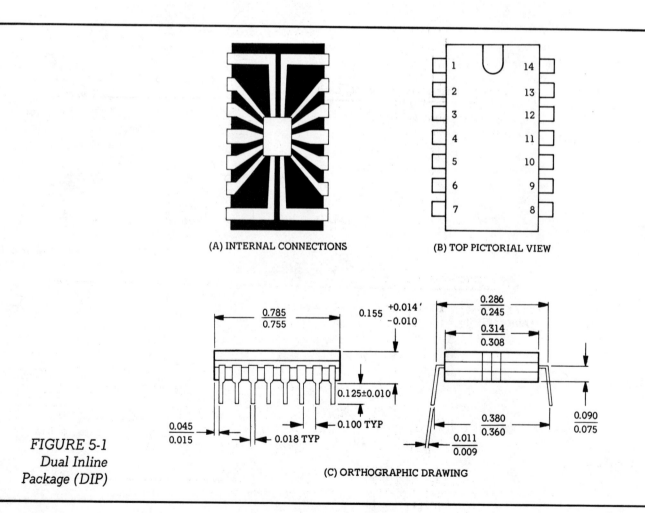

(A) INTERNAL CONNECTIONS

(B) TOP PICTORIAL VIEW

FIGURE 5-1
Dual Inline
Package (DIP)

(C) ORTHOGRAPHIC DRAWING

PLASTIC DUAL IN-LINE PACKAGE TYPE P

**16-LEAD PLASTIC DUAL IN-LINE
PACKAGE TYPE P**

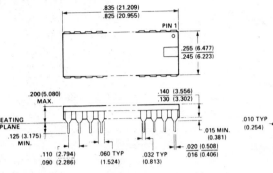

LEADS INSERT ON .100" x .300" CENTERS

**18-LEAD PLASTIC DUAL IN-LINE
PACKAGE TYPE P**

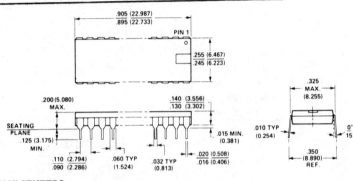

LEADS INSERT ON .100" x .300" CENTERS

**20-LEAD PLASTIC DUAL IN-LINE
PACKAGE TYPE P**

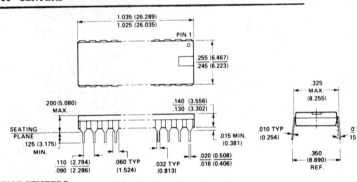

LEADS INSERT ON .100" x .300" CENTERS

**22-LEAD PLASTIC DUAL IN-LINE
PACKAGE TYPE P**

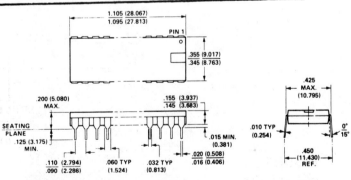

LEADS INSERT ON .100" x .400" CENTERS

*FIGURE 5-1
(cont.)*

PLASTIC DUAL IN-LINE PACKAGE TYPE P

24-LEAD PLASTIC DUAL IN-LINE PACKAGE TYPE P

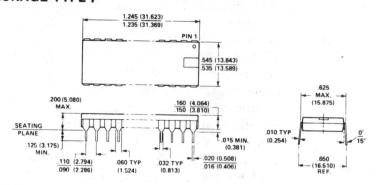

LEADS INSERT ON .100" x .600" CENTERS

28-LEAD PLASTIC DUAL IN-LINE PACKAGE TYPE P

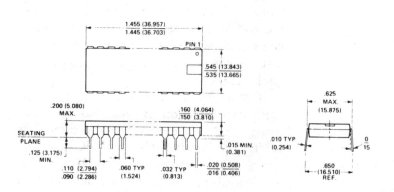

LEADS INSERT ON .100" x .600" CENTERS

40-LEAD PLASTIC DUAL IN-LINE PACKAGE TYPE P

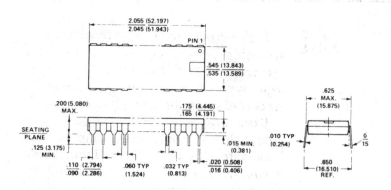

LEADS INSERT ON .100" x .600" CENTERS

FIGURE 5-1
(cont.)

between the output points or the chip and I.C. pins. Then the I.C. is sealed. This process is the same for all I.C.'s made today. (SSI, MSI, and LSI).

Every company that uses IC's in their electronic designs can choose from standard or custom devices. Standard devices are relatively inexpensive and perform some fairly standard functions. Whereas custom devices are specially designed for a specific application and are generally more expensive. Examples of fairly standard IC's are the ones contained in calculators available today or the IC radio you've listened to. An example of a custom device is the IC used in the more scientific programmable hand-held calculators, sophisticated computer circuits, and in some of the electronic TV tuners now available. Both standard and custom devices are used in today's computer technology, as well as in our automobiles and home entertainment equipment.

IC's are by no means magic. They perform as a function of what has been put inside. Today, there are literally thousands of IC types produced by many IC manufacturers. Don't get worried, each IC pack has an identifying sequence of standardized numbers and most manufacturers comply with accepted numbering rules.

Data sheets describe what is inside the chip. All manufacturing companies, especially the larger ones, produce exceptionally good data sheets for their IC devices.

IC's have created a new, more efficient method of designing electronic circuits. Circuits designed using IC's also require the use of symbols to define the circuit to its reader: First for the electronic engineer, second for the PCB designer, then as a tool for the maintenance people to use in the field. Digital logic symbols are, for the most part, unlike those used in the old vacuum tube days. Some symbols used today haven't changed much in appearance and include discrete components used in modern analog circuits such as resistors and capacitors.

Digital logic symbology is unique in that each symbol is itself a condensed map of components. We refer to each symbol as a "gate." Gates perform specific functions within the IC and as mentioned consist of many components (resistors, capacitors, diodes, transistors) previously fabricated onto the IC chip. In most cases, an IC includes many gates. Diagrammed below is the semiconductor integrated circuit building block (See Figure 5-2.)

LOGIC RULES

Basic digital logic layouts use digital symbology; these layouts will be called "schematics." An understanding of digital logic symbols is extremely important to successful layout of digital P.C. Boards.

Basic logic rules apply to gates. Like your lights at home, each lamp has two basic states; *ON* and *OFF*. (A dimmed lamp is considered ON). To *activate* a lamp the appropriate switch is turned on. Likewise to *deactivate* the lamp the procedure is reversed. In the home, 115 volts of alternating current (AC) is used to activate the lamp. When the lamp is deactivated, voltage

is removed and 0 volts of alternating current are supplied. Digital logic gates also have two states and are activated and deactivated by the application and removal of a voltage. But that's where the likeness stops. Logic gates require direct current (DC) signals and in most cases require more than a single action to function. Unlike the light switch above, all that was necessary was one *input* (a flick of the switch lever) to get one output (the light ON or OFF), while each logic gate can require several *inputs* and usually provides one *output*.

For this discussion, an *ON* or Logic 1

state is identified as +5 Vdc and an *OFF* or Logic 0 state as 0 Vdc. 0 Vdc is actually ground potential and is abbreviated GND. This arrangement of +5 Vdc = Logic 1 and 0 Vdc = Logic 0 is referred to as positive true logic, meaning the more positive voltage is a Logic 1. Negative true logic could be used where the less positive voltage is a Logic 1 and the +5 Vdc and 0 Vdc levels could be other values. These rules can be applied to an actual digital logic gate symbol. Figure 5-3 below is what we call the *AND* gate.

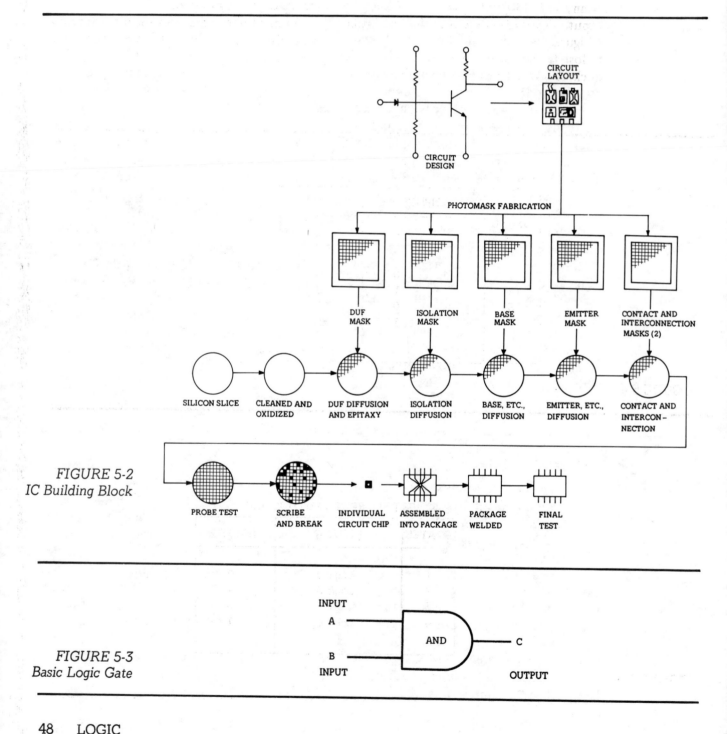

FIGURE 5-2
IC Building Block

FIGURE 5-3
Basic Logic Gate

Leads A & B are *inputs,* Lead C is an *output.* There could have been many more inputs (designated as the fan-in), however, for this explanation only two are used. To make this gate function, we want the output (C) to change state when we make certain changes to the input leads (A and B). Now remember, only two states exist on any one lead whether it be input or output. Figure 5-4 describes the operation of Figure 5-3.

Most IC data sheets provide a truth table which shows all possible combinations of input conditions and the resulting output. For instance, the different conditions that exist for two input leads are shown in Figure 5-5.

As can be seen, a two-input gate can have four completely different input configurations in two-state electronics. With three inputs, there are eight configurations or states, see Figure 5-6.

As mentioned, the data sheet truth table will also provide output states from the various inputs.

STATE	INPUTS		OUTPUT
	A	B	C
1	0	0	0
2	0	1	0
3	1	0	0
4	1	1	1

Where 1 = +5Vdc or Logic 1
0 = 0Vdc or Logic 0

FIGURE 5-4

TWO INPUT TRUTH TABLE

STATES	INPUT A	INPUT B
1	Logic 0	0
2	Logic 0	1
3	Logic 1	0
4	Logic 1	1

FIGURE 5-5

THREE INPUT TRUTH TABLE

STATE	INPUT A	INPUT B	INPUT C
1	0	0	0
2	0	0	1
3	0	1	0
4	0	1	1
5	1	0	0
6	1	0	1
7	1	1	0
8	1	1	1

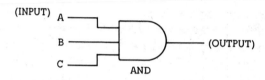

FIGURE 5-6

DIGITAL LOGIC SYSTEMS

Digital logic symbols fall into two categories: basic gate symbols and complex gate symbols. There are three gate symbols in the basic category. These are:

- AND Gate
- OR Gate
- INVERTER

The complex gate symbols include many variations. The symbol used to represent these variations is a rectangular box. Because there are standard and special devices that fall into the complex gate category, all that will be discussed here are the standard flip flop devices. These are:

- Basic flip-flop
  (Commonly known as the RS Flip-flop or latch)
- JK flip-flop
- T flip-flop
- D flip-flop

Special devices that will not be discussed in this chapter include:

- Shift registers
- Counters
- One-shot multivibrator

These devices also use the rectangular box as the logic symbol.

Actually, all complex devices;

- Flip-flop
- Shift registers
- Counters
- One-shot multivibrator

are composed of the three basic gates; AND, OR, and INVERTER even though some data sheets don't show them this way. However, flip-flop packs are widely used to understand their basic operation.

Before we attempt a discussion of logic gate generation, let's review some basic rules:

- There are 3 basic logic symbols; AND, OR, INVERTER.
- All logic gates have at least one input lead.
- Most logic gates have a single output lead.
- The normal Positive Logic convention is:

    An *ON* state is a Logic 1, or High.
    An *OFF* state is a Logic 0, or Low.

- The NAND gate (not AND) is the AND gate with an inverter on the output lead.
- The NOR gate (not OR) is the OR gate with an inverter on the output lead.
- Logic symbols represent circuits within an IC package.
- Each IC package contains at least one logic symbol (hence circuit) usually more.
- The total number of inputs on a gate refers to fan-in.

BASIC LOGIC SYMBOL DEFINITIONS

The AND gate logic symbol is shown in fig. 5-7 along with a dual inline (DIP) IC that includes four 2 input AND gates (called a Quad 2 input AND).

The AND gate shown in Figure 5-7 is a device whose output pin is a Logic 1 when, and only when, all of the inputs are also a Logic 1 as shown in State 4 of the AND Truth Table. When any input goes to a Logic 0 state, the AND gate output also goes to a Logic 0 as shown in States 1-3 of the AND Truth Table. The AND gate can include up to 8 input leads. If only one input is ever used, the device no longer functions as an AND gate. Rather it functions as a buffer element. An analogy to the AND gate is a lamp with two (or more) switches required to turn the bulb *ON*. In Figure 5-8 below, Switch 1 and Switch 2 must be *ON* to energize the light bulb.

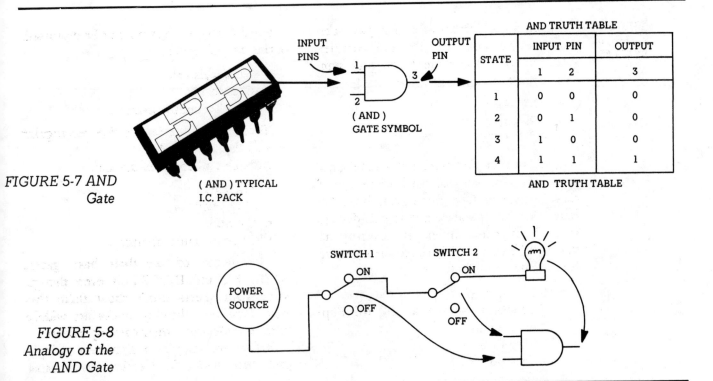

AND TRUTH TABLE

STATE	INPUT PIN		OUTPUT
	1	2	3
1	0	0	0
2	0	1	0
3	1	0	0
4	1	1	1

AND TRUTH TABLE

FIGURE 5-7 AND Gate

(AND) TYPICAL I.C. PACK

FIGURE 5-8 Analogy of the AND Gate

If either or both Switch 1 and 2 are OFF, the light bulb will also be OFF. Therefore, the AND gate is actually a series element. That is, it requires all input states to be *ON* before the output state can be *ON*.

The symbol for a 2-input OR gate is shown in Fig. 5-9, along with a Quad 2-input, DIP or Gate.

The OR gate shown in Figure 5-9 is a device whose output pin is a Logic 1 when any or all inputs are a Logic 1, as shown in states 2-4 in the Truth Table. When, and only when, all inputs are a Logic 0, as shown in state 1 of the Truth Table, will the OR gate output be a Logic 0. The OR gate can include up to ten input leads. If only one input is ever used, the device no longer functions as an OR gate. Rather it functions as a buffer element. An analogy to the OR gate is a lamp with two (or more) switches, where *each* switch can supply power directly to the lamp and light it. In Figure 5-10 below, Switch 1 or Switch 2 or both switches 1 and 2 being on will energize the bulb. The lamp will only go OFF when both switches are OFF.

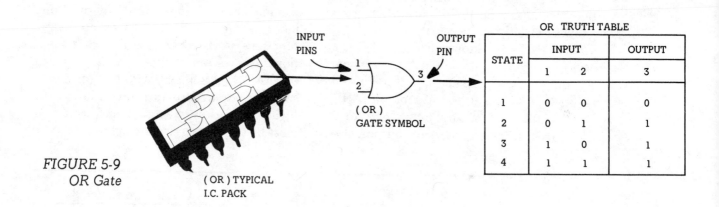

	OR TRUTH TABLE		
STATE	INPUT		OUTPUT
	1	2	3
1	0	0	0
2	0	1	1
3	1	0	1
4	1	1	1

FIGURE 5-9
OR Gate

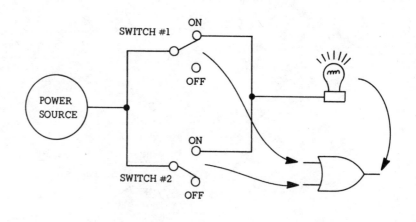

FIGURE 5-10
Analogy of the
OR Gate

Therefore, the OR gate is actually a parallel element. That is, it can be in the *ON* state by any input or inputs or all inputs being in the *ON* state.

The inverter of Fig. 5-11 inverts an incoming signal. Also shown in the Figure is a DIP, Hex inverter (six inverters).

The inverter shown in Figure 5-11 is a device whose output is a Logic 0 when the input is a Logic 1 as shown in State 2 of the inverter Truth Table. The inverter output is a Logic 1 when the input is a Logic 0 as shown in State 1 of the Truth Table. NAND gates and NOR gates as shown in Figure 5-12 below, with all input leads tied together also function as inverters.

An analogy to the inverter requires some reverse thinking. For example, when you turn your lamp switch *ON* you expect the lamp to go ON. If, however, the switch was wired backward the lamp would go OFF when the switch was turned on. The inverter functions this way, when the output state is reversed from the input state.

The Nand gate symbol of Fig. 13 is similar to that of the And gate with a small circle at its output terminal.

The NAND gate shown in Figure 5-13 is actually an AND gate with a "built-in" inverter on the output lead as shown just below NAND GATE Symbol above. The device output pin, as shown in States 1-3 of the NAND Truth Table, is a Logic 1 when any or all inputs are a Logic 0. The NAND gate output goes to a Logic 0 state when and only when *all* inputs are a Logic 1, State 4 on the Truth Table.

An analogy to the NAND gate, like the inverter, requires reverse thinking. An *ON* lamp is normally associated with pushing a button in or flipping a switch *UP*. In Figure 5-14 below, the lamp is always *ON*, powered directly from a power source. Switches 1 and 2 control the power source. As long as Switches 1 and 2 or both are OFF, the power source is not grounded out and it continues to power the lamp. If, however, both switches go ON, the power source is grounded out (the power source is turned OFF) and the lamp goes OFF.

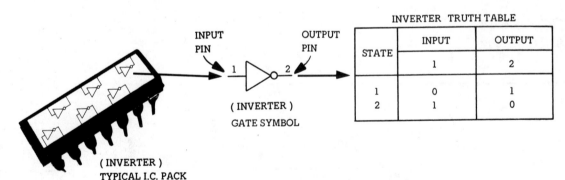

INVERTER TRUTH TABLE

STATE	INPUT	OUTPUT
	1	2
1	0	1
2	1	0

INPUT PIN   OUTPUT PIN

(INVERTER)
GATE SYMBOL

FIGURE 5-11
Inverter Gate

(INVERTER)
TYPICAL I.C. PACK

FIGURE 5-12
NAND and OR Gates Connected as Inverters

Therefore, the NAND gate is a serial element just like the AND gate except that the output is inverted.

The NOR gate Symbol of Figure 5-15 is similar to the *OR* gate with a small circle at the output.

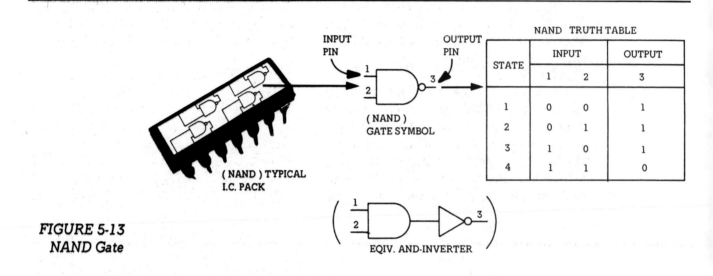

INPUT PIN

OUTPUT PIN

(NAND) GATE SYMBOL

(NAND) TYPICAL I.C. PACK

EQIV. AND-INVERTER

NAND TRUTH TABLE

| STATE | INPUT | | OUTPUT |
	1	2	3
1	0	0	1
2	0	1	1
3	1	0	1
4	1	1	0

FIGURE 5-13
NAND Gate

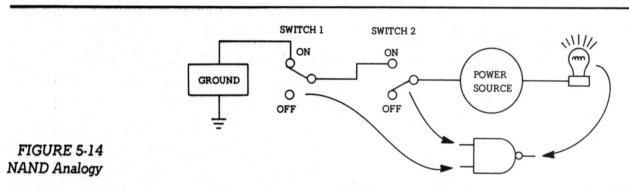

SWITCH 1   SWITCH 2

GROUND   ON   ON
          OFF   OFF

POWER SOURCE

FIGURE 5-14
NAND Analogy

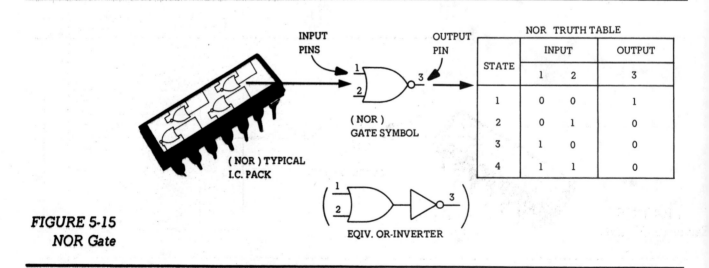

INPUT PINS

OUTPUT PIN

(NOR) GATE SYMBOL

(NOR) TYPICAL I.C. PACK

EQIV. OR-INVERTER

NOR TRUTH TABLE

| STATE | INPUT | | OUTPUT |
	1	2	3
1	0	0	1
2	0	1	0
3	1	0	0
4	1	1	0

FIGURE 5-15
NOR Gate

The NOR gate shown in Figure 5-15 above, is actually an OR gate with a "built-in" inverter on the output lead, as shown just below NOR gate symbol above. The device output pin, as shown in State 1 of the NOR Truth Table, is logically a Logic 1 only when all inputs are in Logic 0 state. The NOR gate output pin is a Logic 0 when any or all inputs are in a Logic 1 state, as shown in States 2-4.

An analogy to the NOR gate, like the inverter, and NAND gate requires reverse thinking. As with the NAND gate analogy, an *ON* lamp is associated with pushing a button *in* or flipping a switch up. In Figure 5-16 below, the lamp is always *ON*, powered directly from a power source. The

power source is controlled by Switches 1 and 2. If a ground is supplied to the power source, the lamp will go OFF. As can be seen, both Switch 1 and 2 are connected directly to a ground. If either switch individually or both are turned *ON*, the power source is grounded out (turned-off) and the lamp goes off. Therefore, the NOR gate is a parallel element just like the OR gate except that the output is inverted.

The Exclusive-OR Gate shown in Figure 5-17 is similar to the OR Gate. The Exclusive-OR Gate output, however, is a Logic 1 when and only when *one* of the inputs is in a Logic 1 state, as shown in States 2 and 3 in the Truth Table below. When all inputs are either a Logic 0 or a Logic 1, the

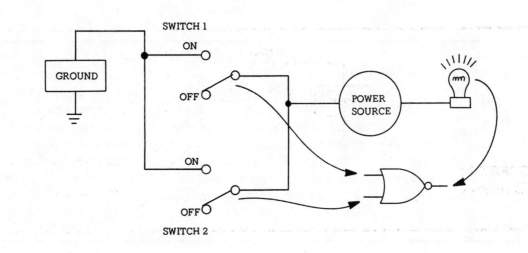

FIGURE 5-16
NOR Analogy

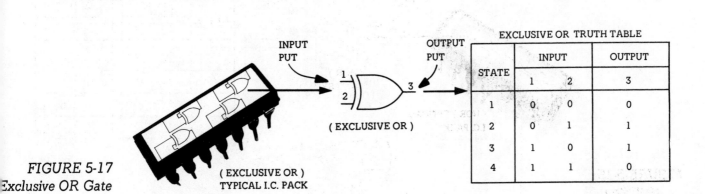

FIGURE 5-17
Exclusive OR Gate

(EXCLUSIVE OR)
TYPICAL I.C. PACK

STATE	INPUT		OUTPUT
	1	2	3
1	0	0	0
2	0	1	1
3	1	0	1
4	1	1	0

EXCLUSIVE OR TRUTH TABLE

THIS IS NOT A STANDARD PRACTICE, BUT MAY BE USED TO IDENTIFY OPEN COLLECTOR GATES

OPEN-COLLECTOR NAND GATE   OPEN-COLLECTOR INVERTER

FIGURE 5-18
Open Collector

Exclusive-OR gate output is a Logic 0 as shown in States 1 and 4 above. The Exclusive-OR gate is therefore a type of lock-out device. It locks out all Logic 0 states at input as well as more than one Logic 1 state.

The logic gates shown in Figure 5-18 above are of the open-collector type. These gates are used in timing circuits, as drivers and for wired-AND functions. If a logic gate is connected to the output of the open-collector gate, it then functions just like a normal NAND gate or inverter. The manufacturing part number is the only means of identifying a open-collector gate from a non-open collector gate.

COMPLEX LOGIC SYMBOL DEFINITIONS

As previously mentioned, the operation of various flip-flop types is important. Devices such as shift registers, counters, and single shot generators will not be discussed due to the vast variety of them. The flip-flop can perform the function of a memory device, a divider, and a counter all in one. It is adaptable to many designs requiring complex logic devices. Like its counterparts, the basic logic gates, the flip-flop is contained within an IC package and in most cases at least two flip flops are available in each package.

The R-S flip-flop is shown symbolically in Figure 5-19.

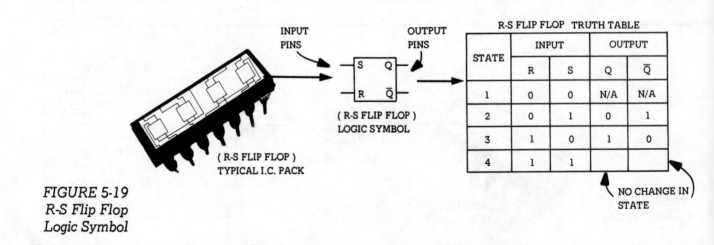

R-S FLIP FLOP TRUTH TABLE

STATE	INPUT		OUTPUT	
	R	S	Q	$\bar{Q}$
1	0	0	N/A	N/A
2	0	1	0	1
3	1	0	1	0
4	1	1		

INPUT PINS

OUTPUT PINS

(R-S FLIP FLOP)
LOGIC SYMBOL

(R-S FLIP FLOP)
TYPICAL I.C. PACK

NO CHANGE IN STATE

FIGURE 5-19
*R-S Flip Flop
Logic Symbol*

The R-S (Reset-Set) flip-flop is the most basic of flip-flops and is generally referred to as a latch. Actually, most latches are a combination of two cross-connected NAND gates, as shown in Figure 5-20 below.

As shown in the R-S Flip-Flop Truth Table, when a Logic 1 is applied to the S input lead (State 2) the $\bar{Q}$ output lead goes to a Logic 1 and Q goes to a Logic 0. When the R input lead goes to a Logic 1 (State 3) the flip/flop changes state; $\bar{Q}$ goes to a Logic 0 and Q goes to a Logic 1. When both R and S inputs are in a Logic 2 state, there is no change in the flip-flop's output state. A Logic 0 state on both input leads is not allowed. Q and $\bar{Q}$ are never in the same state.

Another form of flip-flop is the "D" type shown in Figure 5-21.

The "T" (toggle) or "clocked" flip-flop changes state as a result of an input pulse called a trigger, clock pulse or toggle at the T lead. As shown in the Truth Table, state 1, after the first toggle occurs, the Q and $\bar{Q}$ states change. When the second toggle occurs, the flip/flop reverts back to the original state with Q a Logic 0 and $\bar{Q}$ a Logic 1. If a trigger is placed on the SD lead, the flip-flop goes to State 1. If a trigger is placed on the RD lead, the flip-flop goes to State 2. As long as trigger pulses occur at the "T" input the flip-flop will change state back and forth. Q and $\bar{Q}$ states are never the same.

The J-K flip-flop shown in Figure 5-22 above is an important element in most digital electronic designs. This flip-flop offers complete flexibility in that all possible controls are "built-in" but not all are required for the gate to function. For example, the SD and RD (Set direct and reset Direct)

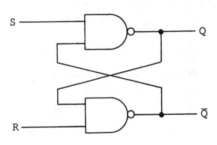

FIGURE 5-20
Schematic of R-S
Flip Flop

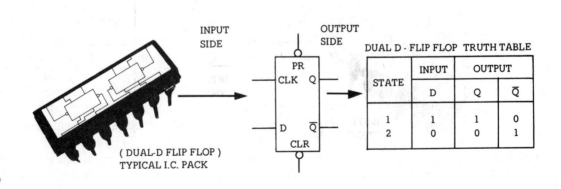

DUAL D - FLIP FLOP TRUTH TABLE

STATE	INPUT	OUTPUT	
	D	Q	$\bar{Q}$
1	1	1	0
2	0	0	1

(DUAL-D FLIP FLOP)
TYPICAL I.C. PACK

FIGURE 5-21
Dual - D Flip
Flop

LOGIC   57

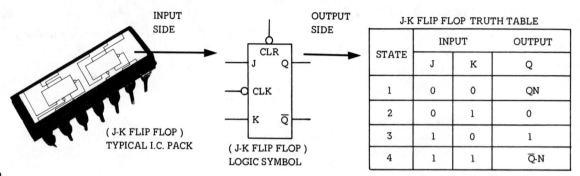

INPUT SIDE

OUTPUT SIDE

(J-K FLIP FLOP)
TYPICAL I.C. PACK

(J-K FLIP FLOP)
LOGIC SYMBOL

STATE	INPUT		OUTPUT
	J	K	Q
1	0	0	QN
2	0	1	0
3	1	0	1
4	1	1	$\overline{Q}$-N

J-K FLIP FLOP TRUTH TABLE

FIGURE 5-22
J-K Flip Flop

leads need never be used. In addition, by tieing the J and K input leads to a Logic 1 state, the flip-flop acts just like a "T" flip-flop already discussed.

As shown in the Truth Table, the J-K flip-flop Q output goes to a Logic 1 when the J input is a Logic 1, as in State 3 of the Truth Table, and a trigger occurs at T. The flip-flop $\overline{Q}$ output goes to a Logic 1, as in State 2 of the Truth Table, when the K input is a Logic 1 and a trigger occurs at T. Therefore, a Logic 1 on one of the input leads while a trigger pulse is occurring

causes the J-K flip-flop output to change state. The J-K flip-flop may have direct set (SD) and direct reset (RD) inputs, in which case a transition from a Logic 1 to a Logic 0 on either lead will cause the flip-flop to attain a certain state. When SD is triggered, the flip-flop reverts to a set state with Q a Logic 1, as in State 3 as the Truth Table. When RD is triggered, the flip-flop reverts to a reset state with $\overline{Q}$ a Logic 1, as in State 2 of the Table. Q and $\overline{Q}$ are never in the same state.

COMBINING

Combining is a term used by the author to describe methods for properly using a logic gate in applications other than what it was designed for. (Substitution might be a more appropriate word). It should be realized, however, that one gate cannot be arbitrarily substituted for another. The rules for combining logic gates as well as some typical design methods used in practice today will be described.

Without first considering the impact combining or substituting might have on the fit, form, and function of your project (be it the repair of a drain pipe, bicycle, automobile, or a printed circuit board layout) you may end up with a real nightmare. On the other hand, *good* combining or substitution habits will undoubtedly result in

the most economical and compact project possible.

A classic example of effects produced by substitution could be; using a spark plug not rated for a car's engine. The negative effects in this case might be poor gas mileage and/or poor engine ignition. Of course the mere fact that an automobile is now running might be a more positive effect. Similar to this example the side effects of substituting logic gates will become obvious during the board test phase. If some very basic rules are followed however, the effects will be positive.

Before attempting logic gate combining, check with the design engineer *and* refer to the manufacturer's specifications. This practice will ensure that gate combining wasn't the cause for the circuit's unsuccessful operation. Be aware of the following characteristics when combining and substituting logic gates:

- Open-Collector Gates vs. Non-Open Collector Gates
- Input Pins and Output Pin Numbers are compatible
- Combining Logic Gates should be done under the Engineer's direction.

To be more specific, combining is a process involving the numbers of logic gate input leads. Before going on, consider this example: If a structure must have four windows minimum to meet your needs having a fifth window would most likely be okay. If it weren't, you could "board-up" the extra window much easier than rebuilding the complete structure. Similarly, if a digital circuit requires a two input NAND gate and a four input NAND gate is available, the spare input leads can be ignored so the gate functions as a two-input device. (Much better than adding a complete IC package). The whole point is to conserve space and save money by using what's available.

Some additional rules to remember follow:

AND - When combining AND Gates, the unused (spare) input lead(s) *MUST BE* connected to *Vcc or to a functioning input lead. (See Figure 5-23)

NAND - When combining NAND gates the unused (spare) input lead(s) *MUST BE* connected to *Vcc or to a functioning input lead. (See Figure 5-24)

OR - When combining OR Gates, the unused (spare) input lead(s) *MUST BE* connected to ground or to a functioning input lead. (See Figure 5-25)

EXCLUSIVE-OR - When combining Exclusive-OR Gates the unused input lead(s) *MUST BE* connected to ground or to a functioning input lead. (See Figure 5-26)

NOR - When combining NOR Gates the unused input lead(s) *MUST BE* connected to ground or to a functioning input lead. (See Figure 5-27)

EXCLUSIVE-NOR - When combining Exclusive-NOR Gates, the unused input lead(s) *MUST BE* connected to ground or to a functioning input lead. (See Figure 5-28)

*Vcc is the positive supply voltage applied

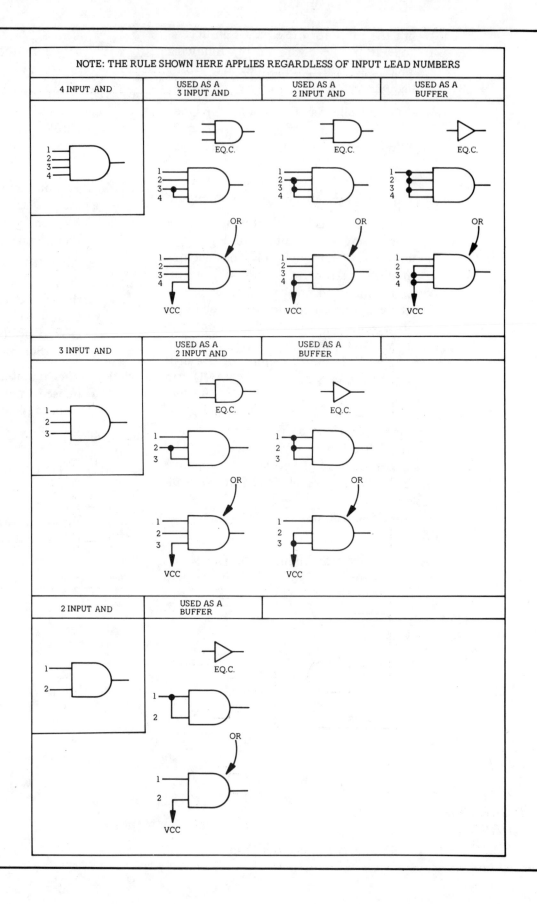

FIGURE 5-23
AND Gate
Combining

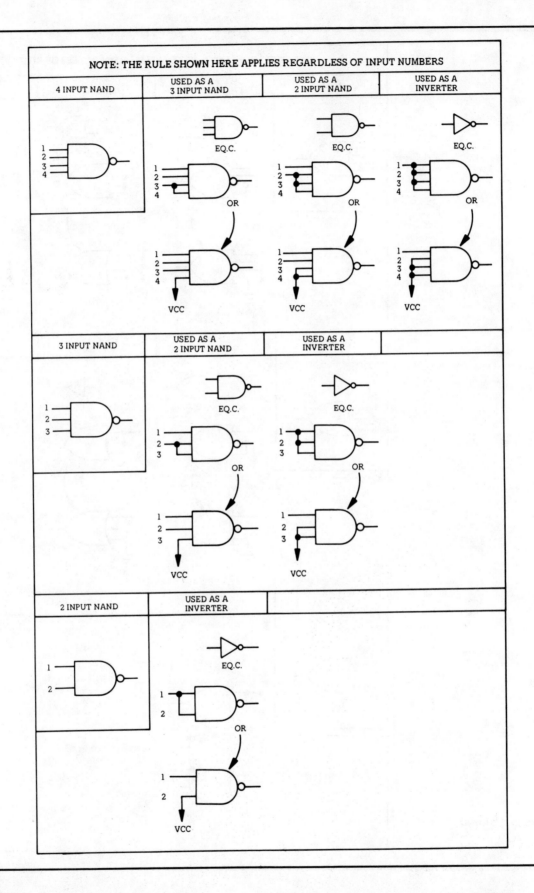

FIGURE 5-24
NAND Gate
Combining

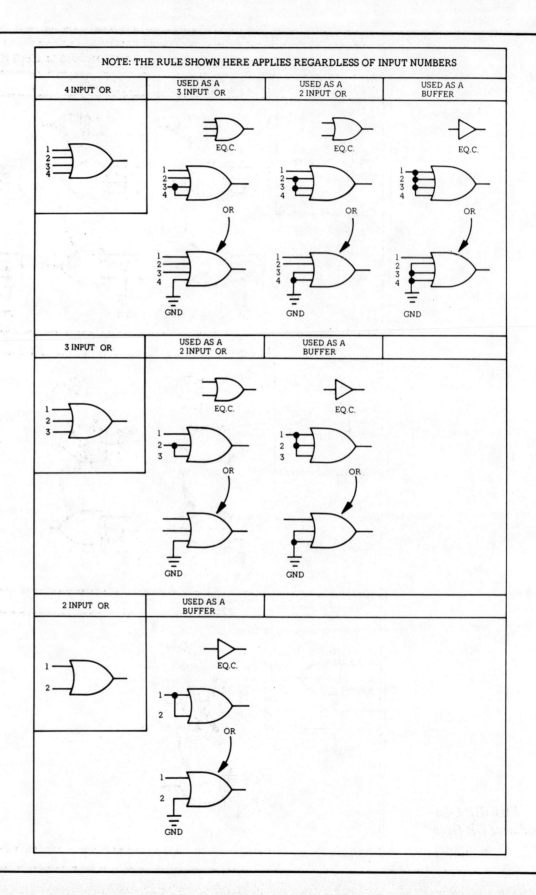

FIGURE 5-25 OR
Gate Combining

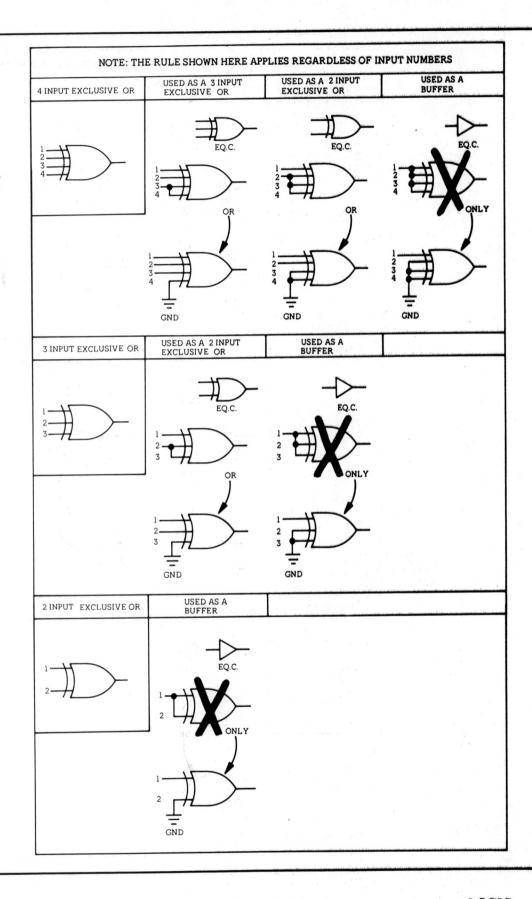

NOTE: THE RULE SHOWN HERE APPLIES REGARDLESS OF INPUT NUMBERS

FIGURE 5-26
Exclusive OR Gate
Combining

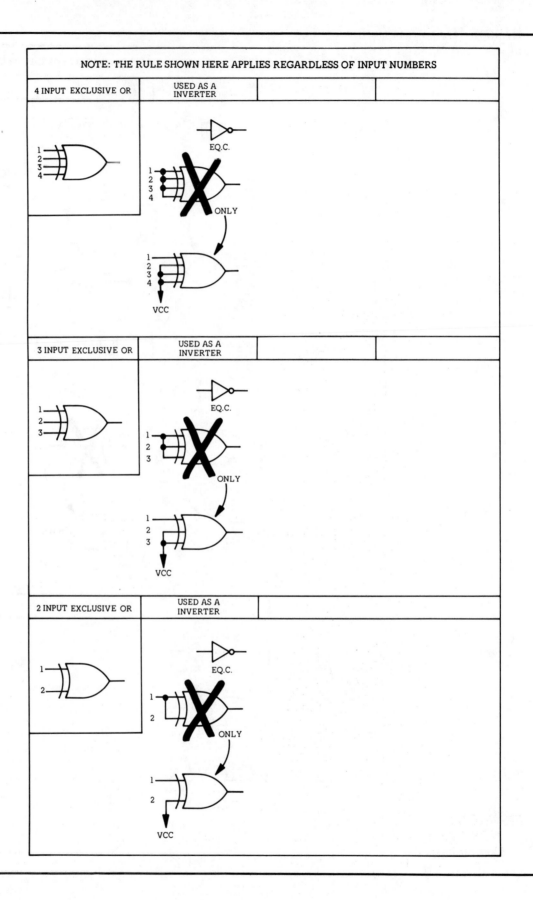

FIGURE 5-26
Exclusive OR Gate
Combining

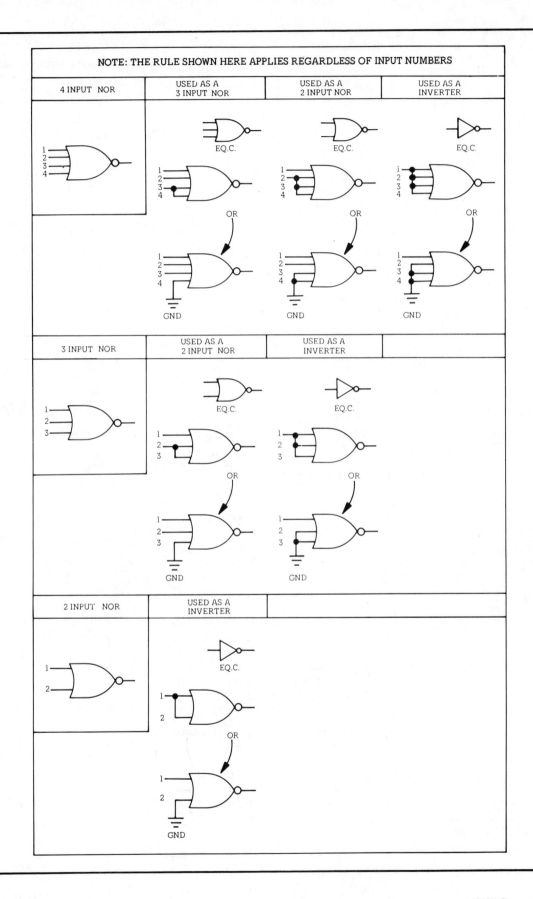

FIGURE 5-27
NOR Gate
Combining

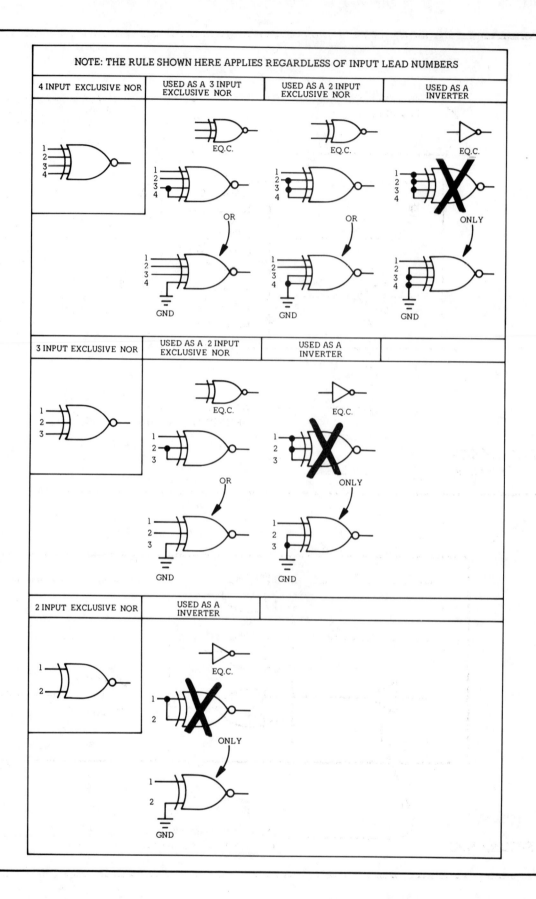

FIGURE 5-28
*Exclusive NOR
Gate Combining*

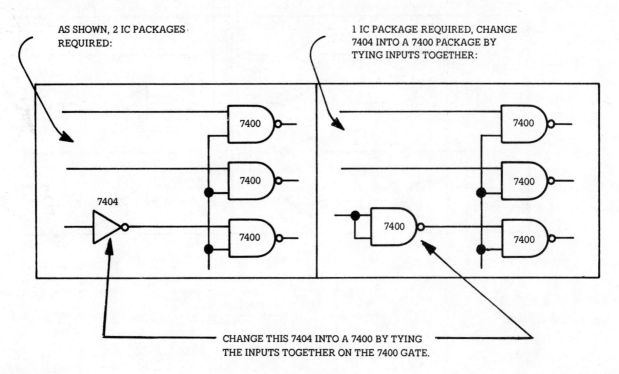

AS SHOWN, 2 IC PACKAGES REQUIRED:

1 IC PACKAGE REQUIRED, CHANGE 7404 INTO A 7400 PACKAGE BY TYING INPUTS TOGETHER:

7400 7400 7400 7404

7400 7400 7400 7400

CHANGE THIS 7404 INTO A 7400 BY TYING THE INPUTS TOGETHER ON THE 7400 GATE.

FIGURE 5-29
Combining

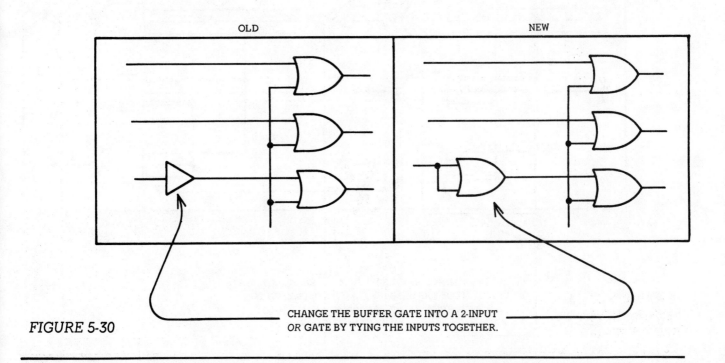

OLD

NEW

CHANGE THE BUFFER GATE INTO A 2-INPUT OR GATE BY TYING THE INPUTS TOGETHER.

FIGURE 5-30

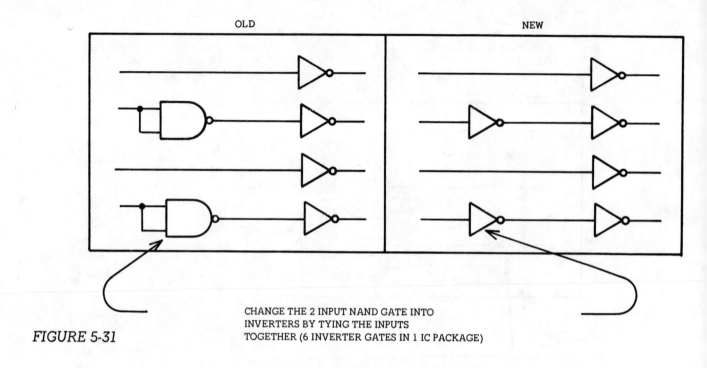

FIGURE 5-31

CHANGE THE 2 INPUT NAND GATE INTO
INVERTERS BY TYING THE INPUTS
TOGETHER (6 INVERTER GATES IN 1 IC PACKAGE)

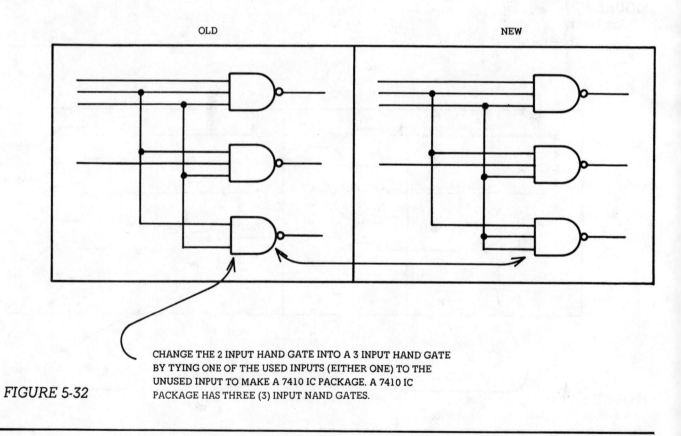

FIGURE 5-32

CHANGE THE 2 INPUT HAND GATE INTO A 3 INPUT HAND GATE
BY TYING ONE OF THE USED INPUTS (EITHER ONE) TO THE
UNUSED INPUT TO MAKE A 7410 IC PACKAGE. A 7410 IC
PACKAGE HAS THREE (3) INPUT NAND GATES.

Chapter

6

INTEGRATED CIRCUIT GROUPING

Grouping digital logic components is a process in which the total number of IC devices required in the design are identified. And once identified the gates are combined to use as many spares as possible, then space is allocated (on a drawing representing the PCB) for each integrated circuit package.

The system sketch, discussed in Chapter 1, could be used for a final PCB layout, however, because it is rough it is highly recommended that time be allotted for a schematic redraw. Using a rough schematic for the layout could result in problems, the most likely of which are listed below:

- Poor PCB design resulting in poor circuit operation.
- Excessive cost resulting from many unused logic gates (too many spares).
- Excessive PCB and Connector real estate required as a result of poor combining, grouping and layout practice.
- Excessive design time resulting from unsuccessful design attempts.
- Excessive time on the street looking for a new job.

It is important that IC grouping be accomplished before the PCB layout has begun. A discussion of this phase follows. It will become clear why grouping is done at the schematic phase and what specific problems can be expected by doing otherwise.

NOTE: Always verify combining of gates with the design engineer. As the PCB designer, you are a recommender. The design engineer should make the decisions.

Identifying the logic gates simply requires a reference to manufacturer specification sheets. This practice is usually done by the engineer, however, this work should be double checked. Reference to these specifications also provides the opportunity to identify the total number of logic gates in each package and the respective gate pin numbers. A table of each logic gate by IC package type should be generated and each gate checked off as it is assigned an actual location on the schematic. In this way, it will be apparent how many spares exist. Figure 6-1 shows a circuit and the IC's assigned by the engineer. The figure also shows a table of each IC package and how each is checked off once assigned to the schematic. Be particularly observant of the spare gates available in each IC package. At this time eliminate as many IC gates as possible. In the example, the two-input NOR IC-5 can be replaced by the two spares of the three input NOR IC-7. Before doing this check with the design engineer for complete compatability. The design engineers may want extra three-input Nor's on the board for future expansion.

NOTE: You have *NOT* assigned gate pin numbers at this point.

Once convinced the minimum number of IC packs are being used, proceed to assign gates to the schematic by area.

Figure 6-2 shows how to assign IC packs by area. This assigning process is done to keep traces short and helps eliminate the need for many PCB feed-throughs. This is where *grouping* plays its most important role. Successful grouping, as shown in Figure 6-2 places the "grouped" gates in close proximity to one another and to connector pins.

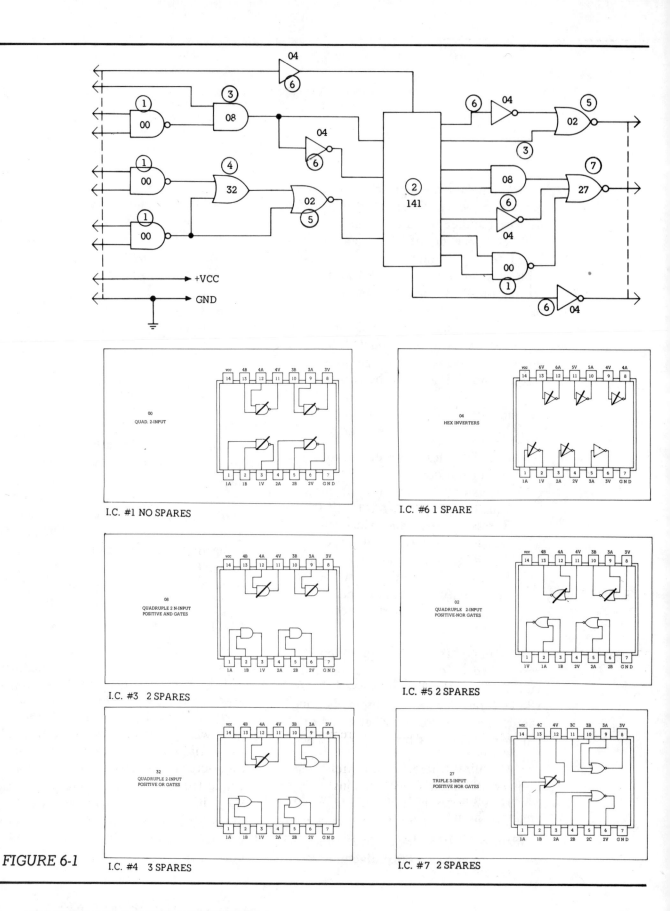

I.C. #1 NO SPARES

I.C. #6 1 SPARE

I.C. #3 2 SPARES

I.C. #5 2 SPARES

FIGURE 6-1

I.C. #4 3 SPARES

I.C. #7 2 SPARES

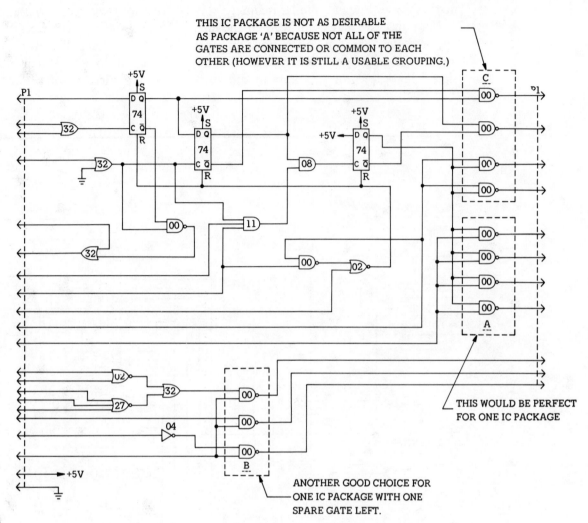

THIS IC PACKAGE IS NOT AS DESIRABLE
AS PACKAGE 'A' BECAUSE NOT ALL OF THE
GATES ARE CONNECTED OR COMMON TO EACH
OTHER (HOWEVER IT IS STILL A USABLE GROUPING.)

THIS WOULD BE PERFECT
FOR ONE IC PACKAGE

ANOTHER GOOD CHOICE FOR
ONE IC PACKAGE WITH ONE
SPARE GATE LEFT.

FIGURE 6-2
Grouping IC's

The rules still apply, regardless of the complexity.

- Determine gate requirements or numbers.
- Combine where possible (referring to manufacturer's specifications).
- Group gates by IC packs to enhance the mechanics of the upcoming design (keeping traces short, close to connectors, while minimizing feedthrough requirements).

Take a good *overall* look at the schematic. Smaller portions are already "grouped" to facilitate signal flow. This flow will determine how the actual PCB is to be laid out. For example, in Figure 6-3 the outputs from both IC 3 and 4 are connected directly into input to IC 2. Likewise, IC 5 outputs are connected to the inputs to IC 6. Furthermore, IC's 3, 4, and 5 inputs come directly from the connector P1. IC 1 and 2 outputs are applied to IC 7, IC 7 and 14 outputs are applied to the inputs of IC's 8, 9, 10, and 11 and so on. This is the flow in Figure 6-3. The schematic should flow in a similar manner.

Undoubtedly, gates will feed to the left, up, or down. These are exceptions, in most cases, and cause no problems in the designed layout, as long as *most* of the schematic is consistent with the proper flow. *Keep the flow in mind and don't be concerned about gates that don't fit the overall left-to-right flow pattern.*

Now that all gates are assigned and grouped look at their placement on the layout. First count the total number of IC

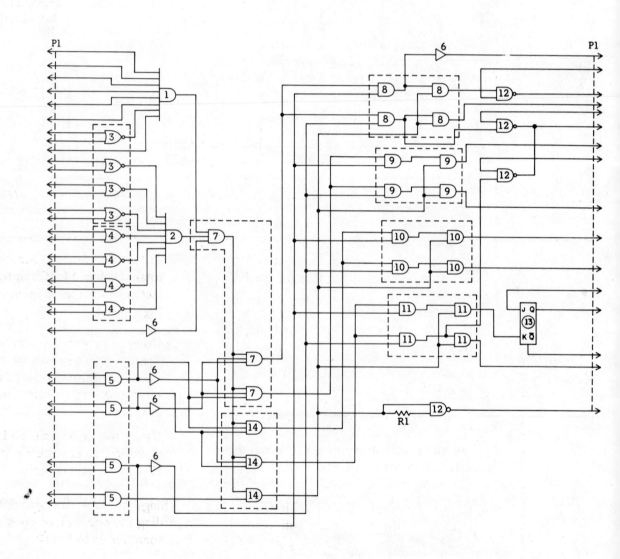

FIGURE 6-3
Logic Diagram

packages; and divide the P.C. board square inches by that amount: For example, if there are 12 IC's on a schematic and we had a 4-in. x 6-in. (4 inches wide by 6 inches high) P.C. board divide 12 into 24 = 2 square inches per IC (See Figure 6-4).

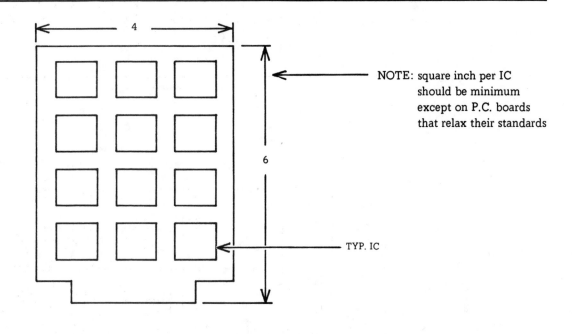

NOTE: square inch per IC should be minimum except on P.C. boards that relax their standards

TYP. IC

FIGURE 6-4 P.C. Board Layout

Now go back to the schematic (Figure 6-3) and try to assign the IC's on the P.C. board.

1. Take a total count of IC's = 14 (using IC spec sheets).

2. Figure total square inches on the P.C. board: 4-in. x 6-in. = 24 square inches.

3. As a rule of thumb, one square inch per IC is minimum for the average P.C. board (use this as a means of figuring the total or maximum number of IC's that can fit on the P.C. board.

4. Count the total number of inputs and outputs to the P.C. board connector to make sure there are enough pins on the connector.

5. Locating the IC's on the P.C. board:

a) A maximum of 24 IC's will fit on the P.C. board.

b) The schematic IC count was 14 IC's total. Divide 14 IC's into 24 square inches = 1.7 square inches per IC (See Figure 6-5).

c) Using Figure 6-5, mark off 5 lines equally spaced horizontally and 3 lines equally spaced vertically. Now at their crossing points, locate 15 IC positions.

Using the schematic and the 15 IC positions, select the positions of the IC's on the schematic.

Things to look for on the schematic regarding the selection of positions on your P.C. board are as follows:

(1) First look at the IC's that go to the connector; they should be placed by the connector end of the P.C. board. In Figure 6-5,

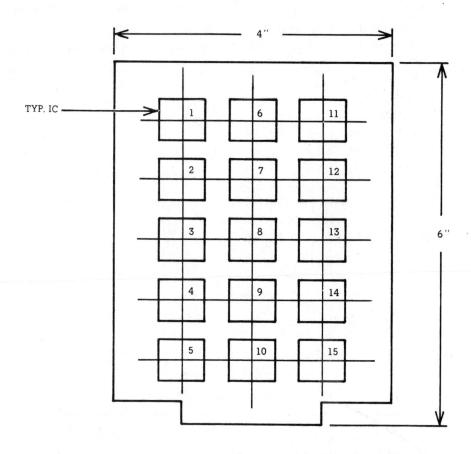

TYP. IC →

1	6	11
2	7	12
3	8	13
4	9	14
5	10	15

4″

6″

FIGURE 6-5 P.C.
Board Layout

positions 5, 10 and 15 are most preferable; positions 4, 9 and 14 are second in preference.

(2) Since the first row of IC's by the connector positions 5, 10 and 15 are selected, the next IC's to be selected are the ones that connect most to positions 5, 10 and 15. First select the IC that connects to position 5 using position 4, and then the IC that connects to position 4 using position 3, position 2 to 3, and position 1 to position 2. Now back to position 10 for the connections from position 9 to 10 and 8 to 9, etc. If there are not any more connections that connect position 7 to 8

and 6 to 7, then stop on that row and go to the next row, position 14 to 15, etc.

6. At this point, go back to the schematic (Figure 6-3) and use the schematic and the IC count of 14 IC's to assign the IC positions to set this P.C. board up (See Figure 6-6).

a. Looking at the schematic (Figure 6-3), IC3, IC4, IC5 and IC1 are the IC's that connect to the connector the most. Select positions 4, 9 and 14; IC3, IC4 and IC5 are placed in these positions respectively (See Figure 6-6). IC1 should be close to the connector also, so we put IC1 in position 3 because it connects to IC3 and the connector.

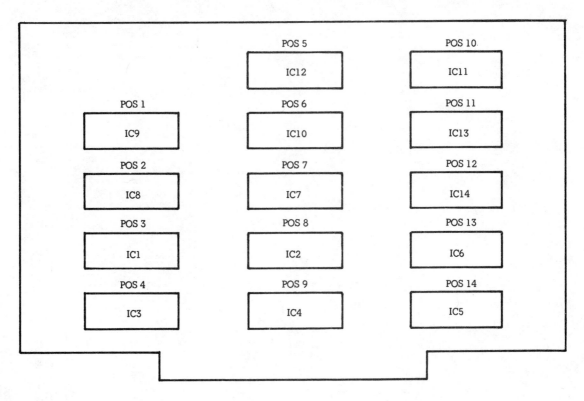

FIGURE 6-6
Final Board
Layout

b. Next, see which IC's are connected to IC4 or position 9. IC2 is connected to IC4 and IC7 is connected to IC2; therefore, position 8 for IC2 and position 7 for IC7 should be selected.

c. Back to the schematic (Figure 6-3) for IC5 or position 14. IC6 connects to IC5, therefore, position 13 should be assigned to IC6. IC6 also goes to IC7 and IC14, which is still close; then IC14 will use position 12.

d. In the schematic the next group of IC's that are common to each other are IC8, IC9, IC10 and IC11, which should be close together using positions 2, 1, 6 and 10.

e. Now the last IC's are out of the common flow. IC12 and IC13 are the last 2 IC's which need positions assigned. First, IC12 connects mostly to IC8, IC11 and IC7, so position 5 would be close to all 3 IC's. Last is IC13, and it should be close to IC11 and would fit very nicely in position 11.

This is just one way to select positions for these IC's; there are several ways and they would probably all be correct. But this will give some idea of how to start and one way to select positions on the P.C. board.

Chapter

7

DIGITAL LAYOUT

The layout and design of digital P.C. boards deals primarily with IC's, which is unlike the analog layout which deals primarily with discrete components.

Figure 7-1 shows a typical digital P.C. board schematic. The layout should begin by using a .100-in. grid spacing along with IC specifications also shown in Fig. 7-1. The board size would typically be provided by the mechanical engineer. For the examples (Fig. 7-3, 7-7, 7-9), the board size will be 3-in. wide and 4-in. deep. (For further detail on board outlines see Chapter 9). This particular schematic has already had the gates grouped. But, before continuing, take time to review the gate grouping of this schematic.

Step 1 IC #1 - The schematic shows 4 NAND gates. Therefore, there would be no spares.

Step 2 IC #2 - Since some IC's are too complicated to show each gate, they are usually represented by a box on the schematic.

Step 3 IC #3 - There are two 08's which are 2-input AND gates shown on the schematic. The spec sheet shows 4 gates available in the 08, therefore there are two spares.

Step 4 IC #4 - The schematic shows one type 32, 2-input OR gate. The spec sheet shows four available. Therefore there are three spares.

Step 5 IC #5 - The schematic shows two Type 02, 2-input NOR gates. The spec sheet shows there are four available. However, there is one type 27, 3-input NOR gate. The spares in the 02 IC cannot be used for the 27, therefore change the 02 gates to 27, which would make three

3-input positive NOR gates on the schematic, leaving no spares available.

Step 6 IC #6 - The schematic shows five Type 04 inverters. The spec sheet shows six available. Therefore there is one spare inverter.

Step 7 Defining the Board Connector Pin Number. If the engineer does not assign pin numbers to the schematic for the connector P1, then the pin numbers are open for selection. The female connector, typically J-1, is the controlling factor in determining the pin number assignment for P1 on the board. Pin number assignments for this board will be as follows:

All odd numbers 1-25 will be on the component side of the board. All even numbers 2-26 will be on the non-component side.

Step 8 Plotting the IC's on the Board Outline. The 3-in. x 4-in. board outline is 12 square inches which means, 12 IC's could fit on this board, if there is one per square inch. The schematic grouped up to a total of 6 IC's. Therefore, there are two square inches per IC available. It would be logical to arrange these 6 IC's in two configurations. Three IC's across with two deep or two IC's across with three deep as seen in Figure 7-2.

The choice between the two configurations is made by the schematic interconnect. If it is determined to interconnect vertically, place the IC's per Figure 7-2a. If it is easier to interconnect horizontally, use Figure 7-2b.

Step 9 - Use the arrangement of Figure 7-2a and set it up as shown in Figure 7-3. Use Figure 7-2b for plotted locations. Looking at schematic Figure 7-1a, IC 1

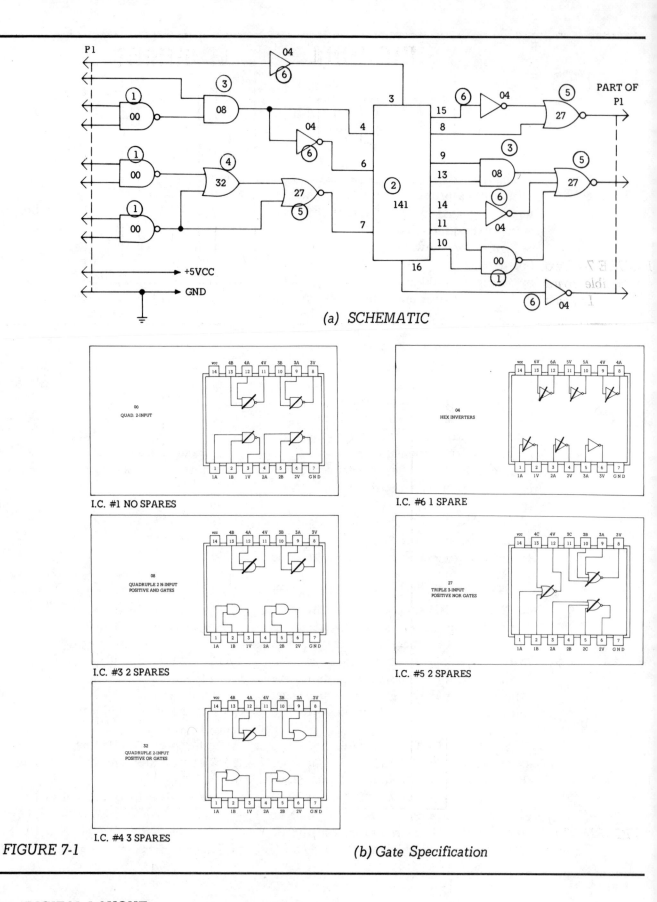

(a) SCHEMATIC

I.C. #1 NO SPARES

I.C. #6 1 SPARE

I.C. #3 2 SPARES

I.C. #5 2 SPARES

I.C. #4 3 SPARES

FIGURE 7-1

(b) Gate Specification

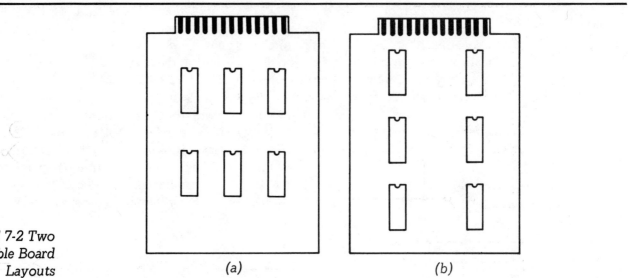

FIGURE 7-2 Two
Possible Board
Layouts

(a)   (b)

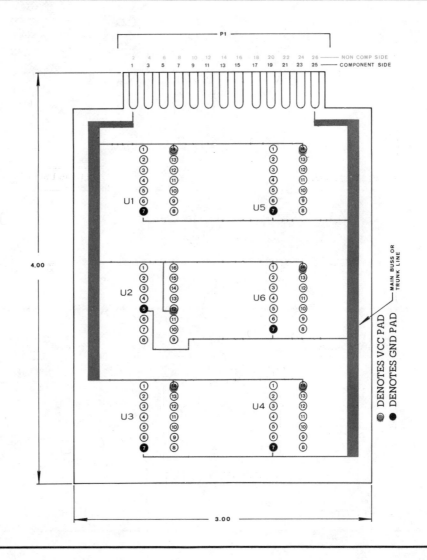

FIGURE 7-3 IC
Layout

and 5 have a lot of connections to P1. Therefore place IC-1 and 5 close to P1. After locating IC 1 and 5, go back to the schematic and try to find which gates interconnect more to IC-5 than any other gates, and which gates interconnect more to IC-1 than any other gates. Establish a chart as in table 7-4 follows using the IC's that have already been plotted. Starting with IC's 1 and 5.

IC-1 should have IC-2 placed below it because it has more connections on the chart than IC's 3 and 4. Likewise IC-5 should have IC-6 below it because of more connectors. IC's 3 and 4 are left. Choose one of these to be placed under IC-2. See Table 7-5 below.

It is obvious from the chart that IC-3 has more interconnections to IC-2, therefore IC-3 should be placed under IC-2. This leaves IC-4 to be placed under IC-6.

Step 10 Identify the Voltage (Vcc) and Ground Pins on IC-1-6 using the spec sheets on Figure 7-1b. IC-1 spec sheet 00 indi-

PLOTTED IC	IC CONNECTED	NUMBER OF TIMES CONNECTED
1	3	1
1	4	1
1	2	2
5	6	2
5	3	1
5	4	1
5	2	1

TABLE 7-4
Tabulations of IC
Connections

PLOTTED IC	IC CONNECTED	NUMBER OF TIMES CONNECTED
2	3	3
2	4	0

TABLE 7-5 IC
Connections

cates that the ground pin is #7 and the VCC is Pin #14. Always use two different colored pencils to distinguish between Vcc and Ground. For example, use red to represent the Vcc pad and black to represent the ground pad. The spec sheets show, that all Vcc pins in this schematic are Pin #14 except IC-2 which is #16 and all ground pins are #7—except IC-2 Pin 5. Now color code them accordingly. Fig. 7-7.

Step 11 - Start putting traces on the printed circuit board. Identify by two different colors which side the traces are on; the component side or the non-component side. Use Pin #1 for Vcc and Pin #25 for ground on P1. Use these pins on this schematic, but they are not necessarily the pins that would be used on other layouts.

Vcc and ground traces are thick traces. The main lines that run down the sides of the board could be even thicker, depending on company standards.

Looking at Figure 7-3, the red pads (Vcc) on IC-1 and 5 are connected with a trace typically min.- of .100-in. thick to the main trunk, which could be thicker. Likewise with row IC-2 and 6 and row 3 and 4. Also in Figure 7-3, black pads (ground) are interconnected on IC's 1 and 5 with a trace that is typically .100-in. minimum to the main trunk, which could be thicker. Likewise with row IC-2 and 6 and row 3 and 4.

Step 12 - The starting point for the interconnection of signal lines (those other than VCC or Ground) is not important. What is important is that the starting point will be the building block from which the rest of the interconnects are based. For example, pick IC-4 which is a type 32, 2-input OR gate (see sheet on Figure 7-6a). Note that on this spec sheet there are four gates to choose, so select one of the four. In the example, select the gate that has Pins 12 and 13 as input pins and 11 as an output pin. Place these numbers on the schematic as shown in Figure 7-6a. This is the beginning of assigning all the pin numbers for

the rest of the gates on the schematic. Decide which three points to connect first. Pins 12?, 13? or 11? In the example 11 is chosen. (It makes little difference which is chosen first). Note that Pin 11 must be connected to a gate called IC-5 (spec sheet - 3-input NOR). The spec sheet shows three gates in this package, select one. Preferably it should be one that is on the same side of IC-4, Pin 11 to simplify the interconnect between IC-5 and IC-4. Also it should be a gate that is close to the bottom of IC-5 because it is closer to IC-4. This is the reason the gate that has input Pins 9, 10, 11 and 8 output is selected. Place these numbers on the schematic. Now Pins 9, 10, and 11 will be interconnected.

Use blue to represent the non-component side of the board which will cross the red color representing the component side of the board. After interconnecting these points on the printed circuit board layout, it is easier to keep track of which points are interconnected on the schematic by using a yellow pencil to cross out the lines as they are interconnected. This ensures no missing interconnects.

Now start interconnecting to another point, preferably a gate that is numbered. For example, IC-4 has Pins 12 or 13 and IC-5 has 8 or 11. Pick IC-5, Pin 11, which is also connected to two other points. One of these two has a number which was assigned, IC-4, Pin 13.

There is now one unknown point to interconnect on IC-1. First, interconnect IC-5 Pin 11 to IC-4 Pin 13. Using the underside of the IC's. This way, is not necessary to overlap the blue lines which were just laid down. Now select a gate on IC-1 to interconnect to the blue line out of IC-5, Pin 11. The closest gate to this line in IC-1 (2-input NAND) would be Pins 9, 10 input, 8 output. Assign this to the schematic and using a feed-through in the second aisle (of Figure 7-7) place it under Pin 8, IC-1. Cross the red line out of Pin 8 with a blue line to the feed-through pad. Next using red,

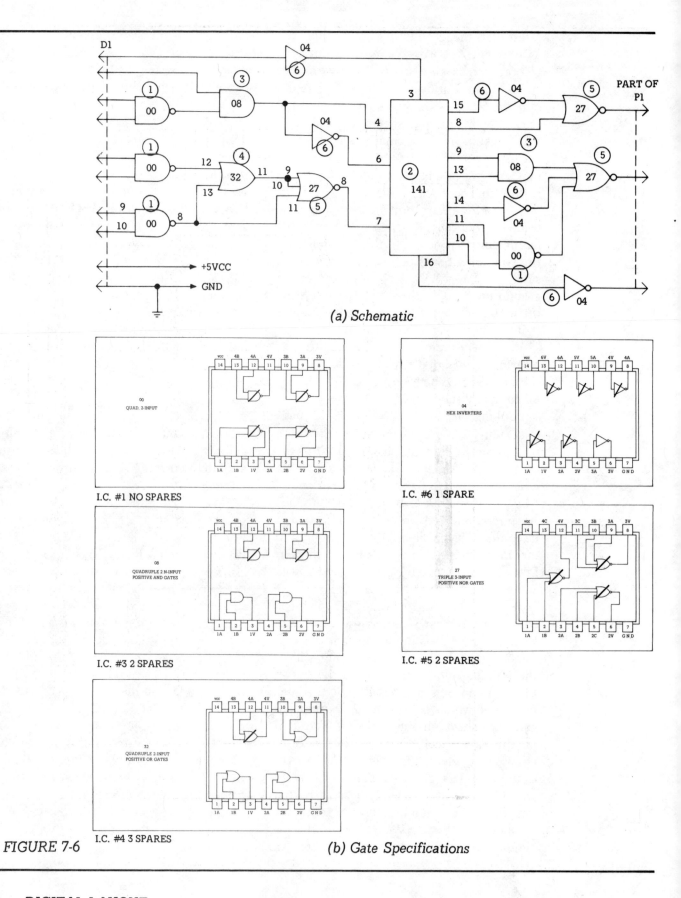

FIGURE 7-6

(a) Schematic

(b) Gate Specifications

I.C. #1 NO SPARES

I.C. #3 2 SPARES

I.C. #4 3 SPARES

I.C. #6 1 SPARE

I.C. #5 2 SPARES

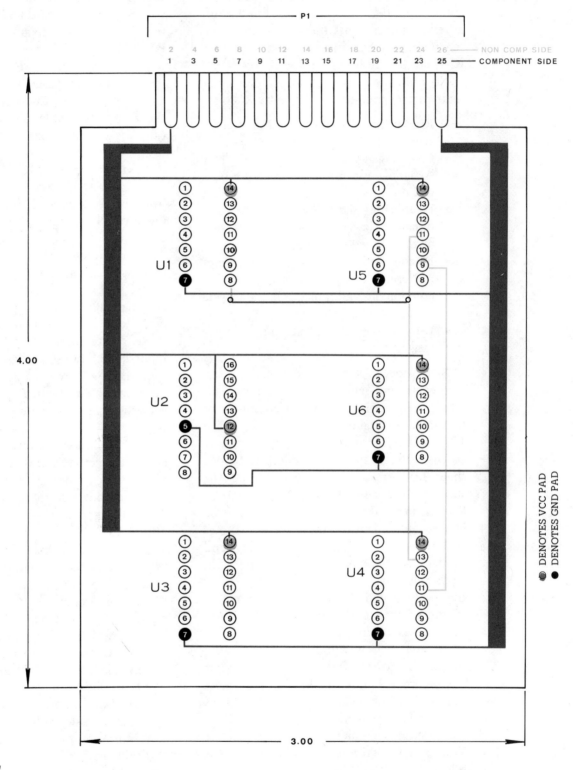

FIGURE 7-7 IC
Layout

draw a line over to the blue line out of IC-5, Pin 11. Now place a feed-through pad connecting IC-5, Pin 11 to IC-1, Pin 8. With a yellow pencil cross out the lines on the schematic interconnecting IC-5, Pin 11, IC-4, Pin 13 and IC-1, Pin 8.

Now that we have given you some insight to the interconnecting phase, such as:

- Establishing board size and connector size.
- Grouping gates.
- Assigning Pin numbers to gate inputs and outputs.
- Establishing signal line colors for component side and non-component side or the printed circuit board.
- Establishing direction of signal lines (different color each side) for the component and non-component side of the board.
- Establishing connector pin number assignment.

Now proceed with the rest of the interconnects using schematic Figure 7-8a with a brief explanation of each interconnect to be shown on Figure 7-9. Connect IC-4, Pin 12, which is the only unconnected pin left on this gate, to an output pin on IC-1 (spec sheet 00 2-input NAND gate). Find the shortest distance between these two points, keeping in mind that an output pin must be chosen. Examination of sheet 00 shows that the choice is limited to Pins 3, 6 and 11 because 8 had been previously used; Pin 11 is selected as shown in Figure 7-9. At this point assign the selected pin numbers to the schematic. Assume from this point on that each time a gate pin number is interconnected, it will be assigned to the schematic. For the following interconnects see Figure 7-9. For the next interconnect put IC-5, Pin 8 to IC-2, Pin 7. Next interconnect IC-2, Pin 6 to an output on IC-6, (spec sheet 04, inverter). To obtain the shortest connection, pick 6 or 8; Pin 8 is selected, making the input side Pin 9. Next interconnect IC-2, Pin 4 to IC-6, Pin 9

and to an output on IC-3 (spec sheet 08). Out of IC-2, Pin 4, the shortest interconnect to IC-3 would be Pin 3. Once Pin 3 on IC-3 is picked it automatically assigns Pin 1 and 2 of the same gate.

Next interconnect, IC-3, Pin 2 to IC-1 output pin. Available pins to choose from are Pins 3 and 6. Choose Pin 6 since it is the closest available pin which automatically assigns Pins 4 and 5 to the input side of the same gate.

Next interconnect IC-2, Pin 3 to an output pin or IC-6. Available pins to choose from are Pins 2, 4, 8, 10 and 12. Choose Pin 2 which automatically assigns Pin 1 on the input side.

Next interconnect IC-2, Pin 15 to IC-6 input side. Available pins to choose from are 3, 9, 11 and 13. Choose pin 3 which automatically assigns Pin 4 for the output pin.

Next interconnect IC-2, Pin 8 to IC-5 input side. Closest available input pins on spec sheet 27 are pins 3, 4 and 5. Choose pin 5 which automatically assigns Pin 3 and 4 to the remaining inputs and Pin 6 to the output.

Next interconnect IC-5, Pins 3 and 4 connect together and then connect to IC-6, Pin 4. Then interconnect IC-2, Pin 9 to IC-3 spec sheet 08 to input and, input side. Available pins to choose from are 4, 5, 9, 10 or 12 and 13. Choose Pin 13 which automatically assigns Pin 12 to the remaining input and 11 to the output. Then interconnect IC-3 pin 12 to IC-2, Pin 13.

Next interconnect IC-3, Pin 11 to an input on IC-5 (spec sheet 27 3-input NOR). Available pins to choose from are 1, 2 or 13. Choose Pin 2 which automatically assigns Pins 1 and 13 to the remaining inputs of the same gate and Pin 12 to the output. Next interconnect IC-5, Pin 1 to IC-6 output side; available pins to choose from are 6, 10 or 12. Choosing Pin 6 automatically assigns Pin 5 to the output side of the same gate. Next interconnect IC-6, Pin 5 to IC-2, Pin 14.

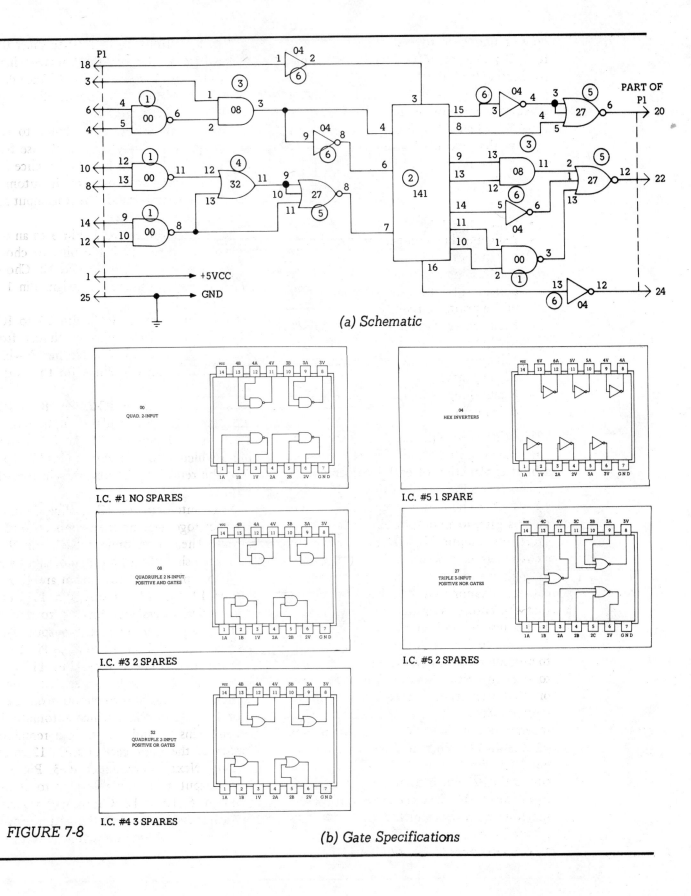

(a) Schematic

I.C. #1 NO SPARES

I.C. #5 1 SPARE

I.C. #3 2 SPARES

I.C. #5 2 SPARES

I.C. #4 3 SPARES

FIGURE 7-8

(b) Gate Specifications

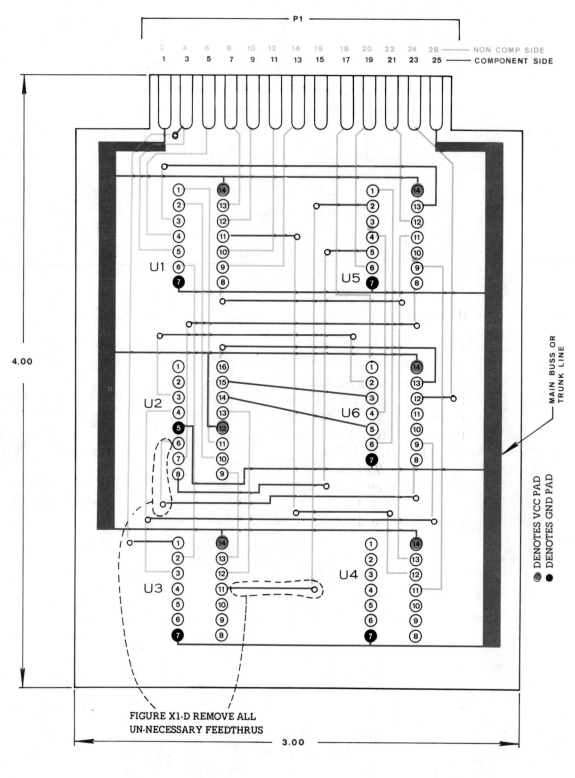

FIGURE 7-9
Final Layout

Next interconnect IC-5, Pin 13 to an output on IC-1. Pin 3 is the only remaining output pin. Which automatically assigns pins 1 and 2 to the input side of the same gate.

Next, interconnect IC-1, Pin 1 to IC-2, Pin 11; IC-1, Pin 2 to IC-2, Pin 10; and IC-2, Pin 16 to an input on IC-6. Available pins to choose from are 11 and 13. Choose 13 which automatically assigns 12 to the output side of the same gate.

The remaining interconnects to be made on the schematic all terminate to the connector P1. In the schematic, P1 does not have preassigned pins for these connections. Therefore as routed the traces from the IC gates to the connector P1, to choose the closest available pin on the odd numbered side or the even numbered side of the connector. Once a pin is chosen, assign it to the schematic.

See Figure 7-8a for the schematic and Figure 7-9 for the interconnections to connector, P1. On IC-1 we have Pins 4, 5, 12 and 13 and 9 and 10 that all must go to the P1. Starting with Pin 5 on IC-1, route 1 - up to Pin 4 on P1. Next connect IC-1, Pin 4 to Pin 6 on P1; IC-1, Pin 13 to Pin 8; IC-1, Pin 12 to Pin 10; IC-1 Pin 10 to Pin 12 of P1; and IC-1, Pin 9 to P1, Pin 14. This connects all the inputs on IC-1 to P1.

Then, IC-3, Pin 1 must be connected to a pin on P1. The closest available pin is Pin 3 on P1. Note on Figure 7-9 that the blue trace we used to route IC-3 Pins to P1 must have a feed-through close to P1, pin 3 to connect to the red side which is the odd numbered side of the connector.

The next connection is IC-6, Pin 1 to P1. The easiest pin to connect to is Pin 18. Following this, IC-5, Pin 6 to P1 is connected to the closest available pin on P1, Pin 20. The next connection IC-5, Pin 12 to P1. The closest available connection to P1 is Pin 22. At this point all the interconnects on the schematic are completed. One of the last steps remaining on the layout is to remove all unnecessary feed-throughs. For examples, see Figure 7-9.

Also, the IC numbers which were assigned in the original grouping of the schematic could be changed to put them in numerical order on the printed circuit board layout. For example, Figure 7-9 has IC-1 in the upper left hand corner with IC-5 to its right. These could be rearranged to have IC-2 in place of 5. In other words, reading from left to right, top to bottom would be IC-1, 2, 3, 4, 5 and 6 or 1 where 1 is, 2 where 5 is, 3 where 2 is, 4 where 6 is, 5 where 3 is, and 6 where 4 is. If the IC numbers are changed as listed, match new IC numbers to the schematic. In other words, when the gates for IC-5 were called out on the schematic, change the 5 to 2 and etc.

Chapter

8

MULTILAYER
P.C. BOARDS

Multilayer P.C. boards are laminated layers of glass epoxy consisting of two external circuit patterns similar in most respects to the standard two-sided P.C. boards, plus one or more etched conductor patterns or layers encapsulated between the two outer layers. These layers are usually connected to the outer layers by means of plated through holes. Boards of this type are used where the system requires a large number of interconnects in a relatively small space.

1. P.C. Boards containing inner layers each composed of a single sheet of copper, commonly called planes. These planes may be a ground plane or voltage plane. Clearance holes are used to eliminate unwanted connections to the plated through holes. Ground planes and voltage planes are particularly useful for P.C. boards mounted with (IC's) integrated circuits or (digital type boards) where these planes provide the power or ground connections.

2. P.C. boards containing inner layers composed of circuit patterns with numerous conductors. P.C. boards of this type are particularly advantageous for highly compacted circuits where space is very important.

Another very useful application for this type of P.C. board is interconnecting other modules or P.C. boards together, commonly called a mother board. In this application, the multilayer board serves as a very efficient interconnection medium since it is light in weight, and occupies little space while also providing mechanical support for the chassis.

3. P.C. boards containing both circuit patterns and Vcc and Gnd planes layers provide the basic advantages of both types and are being found increasingly useful in high density packaging employing numerous IC's.

In addition to the multilayer P.C. board's basic purpose as an electronic interconnecting device, there are other interesting uses for multilayer P.C. boards. Such as a "bus bar," where a large amount of copper on each layer is used to distribute large amounts of power.

ARTWORK   One of the most critical parameters in producing multilayer boards is registration between layers. Proper registration of layers in the finished product depends upon the precision of the artwork or tape-up. This cannot be overly emphasized. The following sequence in laying out multilayer artwork will ensure the good registration.

1. The first layout should be the tooling holes.

2. Two reduction targets and the exact dimension between them should be included.

3. Layout the main component pads or (hole) locations, IC's patterns, resistors, capacitors etc.

4. Photograph (1X1 film positive) the Pad Master same size as the 2:1 tape-up. Now make as many copies as layers.

5. Layout the conductor patterns for the

internal layers first, eliminating any unwanted feed-through pads.

6. Layout the conductor patterns for the two external layers last.

7. Check registration of all layers and clearance for all conductor patterns.

8. The following considerations must be given to assure a satisfactory end product:

a) *Conductor Layout* - Tape of proper widths should be selected to produce the desired conductor width after reduction.

b) *Pads and Hole Layout* - Pads are usually round, although square and special shaped pads are sometimes used, (see hole formula, see page 38) for selecting proper pad size.

Where ground or voltage planes appear as inner layers, the clearance holes required to eliminate unwanted connections to the plated through holes must be clearly marked. This is essential as these are fabricated in the plane prior to laminating.

CORNER MARKINGS

Corner markings and part outlines are essential for the finished product. As a minimum, corner markings should appear on the artwork and tape-up for each layer; these simplify the process.

HOLE LOCATION

There are three methods of locating holes in multilayer boards:

1. Hole location by pad centers or the reduced artmaster or (film). Using this method, all holes are located with reference to pad centers. This method permits the use of optical drilling with holes located directly from the artmaster or (film).

2. *Hole Location by Dimensions from the Tooling Holes:* This method of locating

hole centers is by dimension from Datum lines or X and Y coordinates. When this method is used, the artwork must be carefully laid out to match dimensions which identify hole locations.

Groups of holes may be required to match a specific component pattern such as an IC, TO-5 case or transistor pattern. These holes may be located dimensionally. In locating this type of group of holes, one hole within the group should be designated as a reference hole and located dimensionally to the tooling hole. The remainder of the holes within the group should be located dimensionally to the reference hole.

3. *Hole Location by Grid Pattern:* - Most designers locate hole centers on a predetermined grid pattern. Grid patterns containing increments of .100-in., and .050-in. are commonly used. Listed below are some of the reasons for using a grid.

a) Provides a standard base for spacing and locating component mounting holes, resulting in a simplification of component lead bending where machine bending and trimming is used.

b) Using a grid pattern on the taping is helpful in precisely locating pads on a "pattern to hole" and layer to layer dimensional system (see Figure 8-1).

c) A grid system is often used only for design standardization. Unless a good reason for locating holes to a grid exists, all holes should be located in pad centers. Multilayer boards or any type of P.C. board with holes located to pad centers will have better registration characteristics and cost less to produce, as one potential set of tolerance buildup is eliminated.

HOLE SIZES

A plated-through hole must be sufficiently large to allow the required deposit

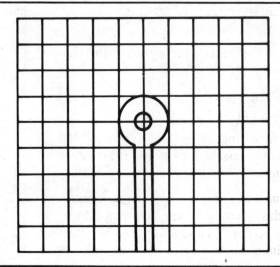

FIGURE 8-1

of metal on the wall. (See standard hole formula, pg. 38). As a rule of thumb, minimum hole diameters should be 3/4 (½ is OK) of the board thickness after plating. This will allow the deposition approximately .0005-in. to .002-in. of metal on the wall of each hole. The metal deposited upon the surface will be up to two times as much as deposited in the hole. Very small holes can be plated-through. However, the ratio of metal deposited on the surface to that deposited within the holes increases.

Round holes should be used in multilayer boards unless a round hole is completely unacceptable because of the shape of some components to be mounted on the P.C. board. Slots, square holes etc., add significantly to the cost of any P.C. board because of the complexity of the operation. Therefore, try to avoid slots or square holes. See Figure 8-2 cross section of a plated through hole of a multilayer P.C. Board.

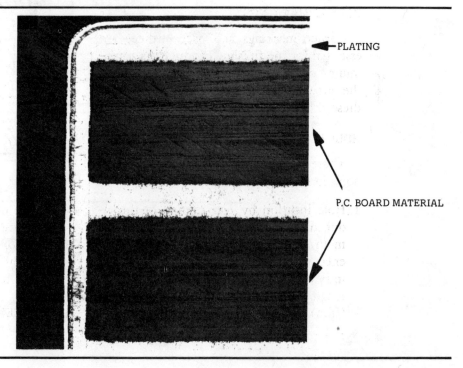

←—PLATING

P.C. BOARD MATERIAL

Cross Section of a plated through hole of a multilayer P.C. Board
FIGURE 8-2

MATERIALS

The base material of the multilayer board should be specified as type "G" grade glass laminated epoxy. The use of these high quality types of epoxy glass as a base material will assure both high stability and minimum P.C. board warpage.

The individual inner and outer layers should have one or two ounce copper clad or a minimum thickness of .001-.0025 inches. (See Figure 8-3). Outside layers should be one ounce copper since the plating adds to the external copper and makes etching more difficult.

"B" stage material: The etched layers will be laminated together using "B" stage epoxy glass cloth. "B" stage epoxy glass cloth is a single layer of glass cloth which has been saturated with a specific amount of epoxy resin. The resin is uncured or partially cured, and will become plastic and flow under the application of heat and pressure in combination.

Usually one thickness of "B" stage material is approximately .004-in. thick before laminating.

However, the base "B" stage materials from the numerous suppliers vary and respond somewhat different to processing methods. Therefore, it is recommended that the final cross section of the multilayer structure be specified and the manufacturer be permitted the latitude of selecting laminating materials which will produce the desired structure. (See Figure 8-4).

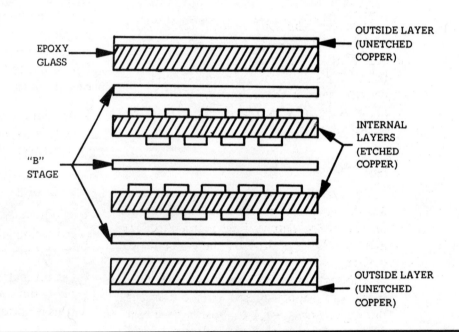

FIGURE 8-3

FIGURE 8-4

LAMINATING

The multilayer P.C. board is produced from a combination of etched internal layers and "B" stage materials after the application of heat and pressure are applied (See Figure 8-3). Laminating is one of the more critical processes in producing a multilayer P.C. board. The structure must be totally free from voids and this can be done only by a complete adherence of the epoxy resin throughout the conductor patterns and glass fibers on the inner layer. Two ounce copper, for example, requires a larger amount of resin to fill the voids around the conductor patterns than does one ounce. Similarly, three ounce copper requires more.

Suppliers of these materials such as "B" stage and the base material differ somewhat resulting in slight variations in the end products.

However, the end product must be a multilayer P.C. board having a total thickness of no more than specified on the blueprint. Thus, it is recommended that the designer permit the manufacturer a degree of latitude in selecting the base and "B" stage materials.

PLATING

On plated-through holes on multilayer boards, copper is the first metal deposited on the walls. During hole plating, copper may also be deposited on the entire board surface.

Although some P.C. boards are produced with only copper plated circuit patterns, the big majority of P.C. boards have conductors plated with a second metal or alloy. This could be done for a number of reasons, such as to prevent corrosion of the copper, or to improve the solderability, etc.

CUTTING TO FINAL SIZE AND SHAPE

To facilitate production and handling, one sheet (see Figure 8-3 and 8-4) may actually contain many final boards.

Various methods are used to cut multilayer P.C. Boards to their final size and shape. For small to medium quantities, routing to size and shape is the most common; and parts thus produced will be within ± .010-in. of the specified dimension.

P.C. BOARD THICKNESS

On multilayer boards designed with fingers or edges intended for insertion into connectors, the board thickness is important. To meet the requirements of most commercially connectors, the P.C. board thickness should be specified ± .007-in. of the nominal thickness specified. This is standard tolerancing.

FABRICATION DRAWING

Possibly the most important consideration for accurate and economical production of multilayer P.C. boards is the initial preparation of a correct and complete fabrication drawing.

The information contained on the fabrication drawing should be as follows:

1. An outline drawing of the part or P.C. boards showing all dimensions and tolerances.

2. A description of the base material G10 or G10FR - or other selected material.

3. A cross-section of the desired end item indicating all layers (by number) and critical dimensions. (See Figure 8-4).

4. Circuit pattern images for non component side identified by layer number (this is optional) but very desirable.

5. Thickness of copper, by layer, taking into consideration the plated through hole process which will increase the copper thickness of the outside layers.

6. A table showing hole diameters, tolerances and number of holes, and a coding system so that holes shown in the hole table can be identified on the multilayer circuit board. (See Figure 8-5).

Hole	Quantity	Diameter	Tolerance
A	2	.375	± .005
B	13	.093	± .002
C	7	.125	± .003
D	All other	.040	± .003

FIGURE 8-5

7. A note or code stating which holes are plated through.
8. Any nomenclature or markings other than the circuit pattern.
9. Name and number of any other specifications that may apply to the part.

Figure 8-6 and 8-7 show a plated through connection between external pads and one internal layer. This provides clearance at the other layer.

A. Dimension denotes pad size.
B. Dimension denotes hole size.
C. Dimension denotes clearance around hole.

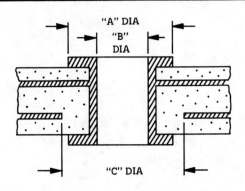

FIGURE 8-6

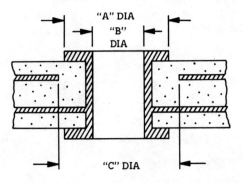

FIGURE 8-7

Figure 8-8 provides a plated through clearance hole through the board for mounting components or a feed through hole.

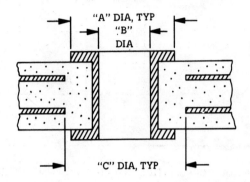

"A" DIA, TYP

"B" DIA

"C" DIA, TYP

FIGURE 8-8

TYPICAL CODING METHOD FOR
A MULTILAYER P.C. BOARD:

1. All pads connected to ground shall be symbolized as shown ⊗ or color code these pads.

2. All pads connected to Vcc shall be symbolized as shown ⊖ or color code these pads.

3. Color of each layer will denote connection.

Chapter

9

BOARD OUTLINE

Before a printed circuit board is started (locating the components and traces), several items must be defined. One of the first is the working board area; as shown in Figure 9-1.

The following items are some of the considerations that should be involved prior to starting the actual circuit packaging:

1. What type of housing or enclosure will the completed board assembly be mounted in?

2. What method of fastening or mounting the board is best for this application (card guides, screws, standoffs, etc.)?

3. What type of electrical interface is available (connector, cable, wires, etc.)?

4. Will the board require card extractors or special extractor tools to aid in removal of board from enclosure?

5. If board is large or irregular in shape, are stiffeners or special braces required?

These questions and others that are typical to any number of design requirements are covered in the following outline.

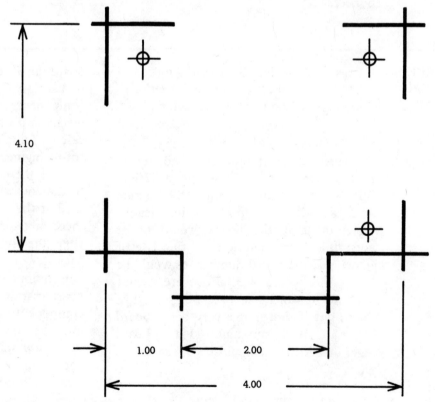

FIGURE 9-1
Board Outline NOTE: All dimensions ±.02-in.

BOARD OUTLINE   Depending on how the P.C. card mounts or slides into the next assembly, the configuration of the board must be such that it clears any obstacles or interferences. Therefore, a typical board may have cutouts, radiuses or other irregular shapes. It is important to remember that every cut, hole or routing operation that is used increases the cost of the board. To minimize cost keep the configuration as close to a basic square or rectangle as possible.

METHOD OF MOUNTING   If the type of electrical interface requires the P.C. card to insert into a mating connector, then card guides offer the most convenient solution. They not only provide a quick "connect/disconnect" capability, but also provide a means of testing the board out of the unit by means of extender cards. One of the most economical ways to provide this type of interface is by the use of an edge connector. This method not only eliminates the cost of buying an additional connector, but saves manufacturing time by not having to assemble that second connector.

If the electrical interface is by means other than a connector or a card guide is not practical, then mounting holes must be included on the board so that it can be installed with screws, standoffs or other mechanical fasteners.

Whatever means is decided upon, sufficient clearance should be provided so that components or conductors will not interfere or short out to the mounting hardware.

WORKING BOARD AREA   Regardless of the board configuration, a few basic rules must be considered prior to beginning the component packaging phase.

1. *Tolerance* - All board outlines must be expressed to include some tolerance. Most common are ±.010- and ±.020-in. This is important because the actual working board area must be the smallest dimension that the board would be at worst tolerance condition. In the case of Figure 9-2, the board dimensions would be 8.08 x 4.03 inches or 32.56 square inches. That .02-in. tolerance may not seem like much; but if designing a very dense board where a trace runs within .040-in. of board edge, that tolerance could be of significant value.

2. *Component Interference* - If the P.C. board mounts into an enclosure that has an interference or obstacle near the board area, careful planning must insure that the P.C. board assembly (including components and hardware) will not have mechanical or electrical interference. In the case of some critical R.F. circuits, the electrical engineer must approve the relationship of the components on the P.C. board to the environment that they will be packaged at the final assembly. Closeness to the sheet metal chassis or other circuits could alter the function of the circuit being packaged.

Component interference is also a major consideration within the P.C. board. All components, heat sinks, fasteners, etc., must be considered on the layout at their *maximum size* or greatest area of interference. This is especially critical in considering such components as special designed transformers, chokes, etc., because the prototype device that may be provided as a sample sometimes grows in size between

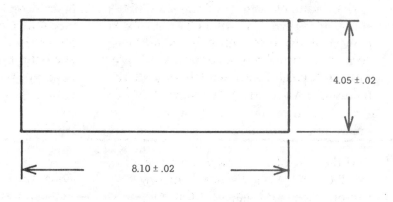

4.05 ± .02

8.10 ± .02

FIGURE 9-2
Working Board
Area

the prototype stage and the final production of that particular part. If there is no data sheet or reliable specification on any given part or component, leave adequate space to include maximum interference area of that part.

3. *Method of Mounting Board at Next Assembly* - There are various methods available to secure the board assembly to the next assembly. The application best suited for the particular board must be decided prior to starting board layout. This is important because if standoffs are used to mount the board, make sure that components or traces will not be in the position where a hole is drilled or a fastener is installed. In the case of card guides, sufficient area would have to be left clear to allow room for the card guide along the edge of the board.

Other items associated with the board mounting are items such as: Card ejectors, mounting holes, stiffeners, and metallic or non-metallic card guides (If card guides are non-metallic, traces may be routed right out to the edge of the board).

One basic consideration on *all* printed circuit packaging is the leads that protrude through the non-component side of the printed circuit board. Adequate clearance must be provided for all leads, wires, hardware, etc. to ensure they will not short out to an adjacent board, sheet metal or object mounted underneath the board. The allowance for these leads is generally not to exceed .060- to .100-in.; therefore, a minimum clearance of an additional .060- to .100-in. should be designed into the mechanical package. If the board is an exceptionally large board or made of thinner material, it might require even additional clearance to ensure that flexing of the board under vibration or stress would not allow the leads to short out.

INTERFACE CONNECTIONS

One of the basic requirements of any P.C. board is to provide means of electrical interface between the board and its associated equipment. The most common method of accomplishing this is by the use of connectors, terminals and/or cables.

1. *Connectors* - The type of connector or interface that will be used for any particular board is generally decided upon during the mechanical design of any given piece of equipment. This is necessary because not only does the P.C. board have to consider the type of connector or connection, but the associated mechanical package must provide space for the connector or connection that will mate with the printed circuit board. The choice of connectors that are available are too numerous to cover, but there are models and configurations to fit almost any requirement.

2. *Terminals* - Connectors have the advantage of a quick connect-disconnect, but in some applications terminals would be a convenient interface method to choose. In applications that require low volume production or applications where the P.C. board is not apt to be removed, there is no reason to go to the expense of installing a connector. Terminals are also an advantage in cases where a design will have models that are the same basic circuit but require input connectors to be different from model to model.

The type of cable best suited for any given board is greatly dependent on the electrical requirements and/or contract mandates. Cables, in general, range from a few single wires (bundled together and connected from unit to unit) to cable assemblies that are massive in diameter.

PRINTED CIRCUIT BOARD MATERIALS

Materials for P.C. boards generally fall within a couple of standard laminate grades with "G-10" and "FR-4" being the most common due to the availability of the material. Table 9-1 lists these laminates.

Although the laminates range in a variety of material, the finished P.C. board material (laminate with copper applied) is generally treated the same as far as etching the final printed circuit board.

Grade	Composition	Remarks
XXXPC	paper / phenolic	High moisture resistance
FR-2	paper / phenolic	Similar to XXXPC but flame retardant
XXXP	paper / phenolic	Best mechanical characteristics of paper / phenolic grades
FR-3	paper / epoxy	High mechanical and electrical characteristics, flame retardant
FR-4	glass / epoxy	Flame retardant, chemical resistant, low water absorption
G-3	glass / phenolic	High flexural strength and dimensional stability
G-5	glass / melamine	High resistance, high impact strength
G-9	glass / melamine	Same as G-5 but better electrical characteristics
G-10	glass / epoxy	Same as FR-4 but not flame retardant
G-11	glass / epoxy	Same as G-10 but higher flexural strength under heat
G-30	glass / polymide	High demensional stability under heat, flame retardant
FR-5	glass / epoxy	Same as G-11 but flame retardant
GPO-1	glass / polyester	General purpose mechanical and electrical grade
GPO-2	glass / polyester	Similar to GPO-1 but lower flammability

TABLE 9-1 Major Laminate Grades Used by P.C. Suppliers

TOOLING HOLES

Tooling holes are used as P.C. Board reference points upon which other dimensions are based. These are noted in Figure 9-3.

During the manufacturing process, the manufacturer will "tool-up" or design his fixtures for drilling the P.C. board using these tooling holes as a reference point. It is, therefore, necessary that the dimensions in reference to the tooling holes be located accurately per the dimensions given on the fabrication drawing.

In cases of very dense boards, there may not be sufficient room on the board to locate the pads for the tooling holes; therefore, it will be necessary to locate them outside the perimeter of the board outline. They will appear on the final positive and negative film which the manufacturer will use to produce the board. The same accurate dimensioning would still apply, but after the board is completed, they would be trimmed away with the other excess material.

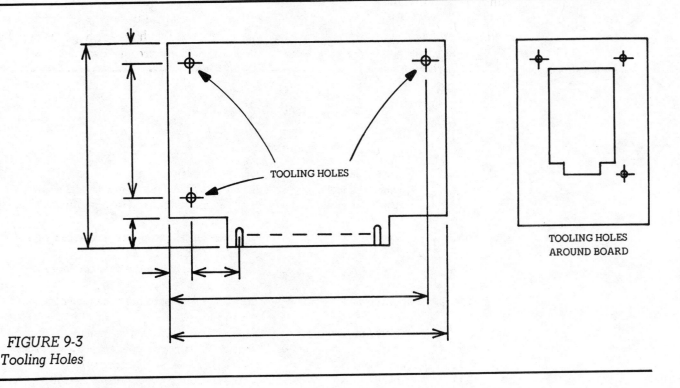

TOOLING HOLES

TOOLING HOLES
AROUND BOARD

FIGURE 9-3
Tooling Holes

Chapter

10

PRODUCTION CONSIDERATIONS

**MECHAN-
ICAL
INSERTION**

Designing P.C. boards for mechanized component insertion reduces board assembly cost. To get the best savings from automatic insertion machines, P.C. board designs should accommodate the special requirements and specify components of this technique.

**BEST
COMPONENT
ARRANGE-
MENT**

The most economical axial lead component arrangement for mechanized component assembly is one in which all components are identical, all lead spans are the same, and all component bodies are oriented in the same direction. This arrangement is one of the lowest cost methods because the components can be fed directly from a supplier's tape reel to a standard insertion head and directly into the P.C. board that has only to be put into the machine and taken out once.

However, an axial lead component arrangement that is best for automatic assembly is rarely best from a functional design standpoint; so most P.C. boards are a compromise of these two needs.

One of the best component arrangements is shown in Figure 10-1 where all lead spans are the same and all the component cases (or bodies) are oriented in same direction. This arrangement will give an assembly cost factor of 1.00, based on insertion costs with a machine having a manually variable center distance insertion head. Sequencing costs are included because few P.C. boards have components that are all electrically alike.

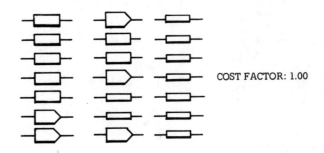

COST FACTOR: 1.00

*FIGURE 10-1
Same Lead Spans,
Same Direction*

Figure 10-2 is a compromise arrangement; the different components still are oriented in the same direction, but the sequenced parts have two or more different lead spans. This difference increases the machine assembly cost factor to 1.05. This is still an acceptable cost compromise.

Another compromise arrangement is Figure 10-3 which has two or more different lead spans and six of the components are oriented 90 degrees to the others. Having two orientations increases the cost factor to 1.25. This is also an acceptable compromise.

In the compromise of Figure 10-4, seven of the components are oriented 90 degrees to the others, and the components in each group are scattered around the P.C. board. Also, each group has three different lead spans which adds to the cost. The cost factor here is 1.35; this may be very close to an undesirable compromise.

This could be undesirable because of the excessive machine traverse time required to insert similarly oriented components that are scattered around the P.C. board. The most economical use of the automatic machine dictates that all components with the same orientation be inserted before the board is re-positioned for another orientation. In this case, the machine has to be stopped six times to manually change the

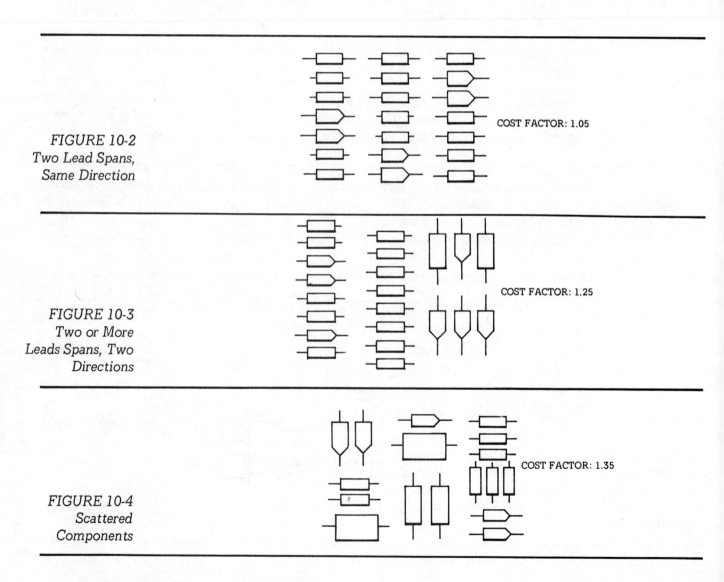

FIGURE 10-2
Two Lead Spans,
Same Direction

COST FACTOR: 1.05

FIGURE 10-3
Two or More
Leads Spans, Two
Directions

COST FACTOR: 1.25

FIGURE 10-4
Scattered
Components

COST FACTOR: 1.35

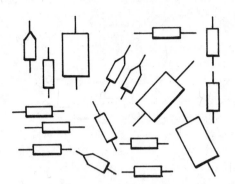

FIGURE 10-5
Unacceptable
Layout for Low
Cost Automatic
Insertion

insertion head for each of the six different lead spans. However, even with the scattered components, this layout would be acceptable with a cost factor of 1.35.

This arrangement of figure 10-5 is totally impractical; there are too many different component orientations which result in excessive idle machine time while the board is being realigned to the insertion head for each of the orientations. The requirement to hold the board at a number of different angles to the insertion head increases the tooling cost. Cost factors of the example in Figures 10-1 through 10-5 have assumed insertion with a manually variable head. Actually, many insertion machines are in use today not only fixed heads, but heads that can be switched back and forth between two lead spans. Effective use of these machines requires even closer evaluation of component arrangement.

AXIAL COMPONENT ARRANGEMENTS
One approach to automatically insert transistors with radial leads is the axial method shown in Figures 10-6 and 10-7. The transistors inserted in this fashion are sequenced on tape and inserted with a machine having a modified axial lead component head.

The best arrangement for axially inserted transistors in a specific sequence is one lead span and one orientation such as Figure 10-6. This arrangement could be considered to have a machine assembly cost factor of 1.00. The second arrangement (Figure 10-7) cost factor has increased to 1.25 because of changing the orientation.

By preforming leads in Figure 10-8 components with radial leads can be processed like axial lead posts in automatic insertion machines.

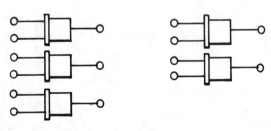

FIGURE 10-6
Transistor Layout

COST FACTOR: 1.00

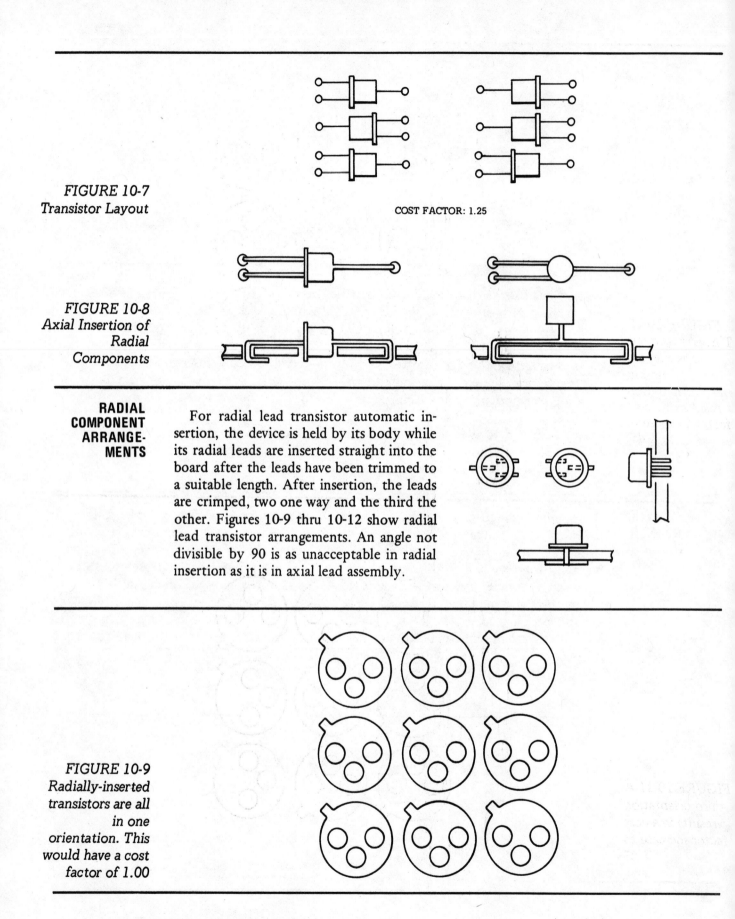

FIGURE 10-7
Transistor Layout

COST FACTOR: 1.25

FIGURE 10-8
Axial Insertion of
Radial
Components

**RADIAL
COMPONENT
ARRANGE-
MENTS**

For radial lead transistor automatic insertion, the device is held by its body while its radial leads are inserted straight into the board after the leads have been trimmed to a suitable length. After insertion, the leads are crimped, two one way and the third the other. Figures 10-9 thru 10-12 show radial lead transistor arrangements. An angle not divisible by 90 is as unacceptable in radial insertion as it is in axial lead assembly.

FIGURE 10-9
Radially-inserted
transistors are all
in one
orientation. This
would have a cost
factor of 1.00

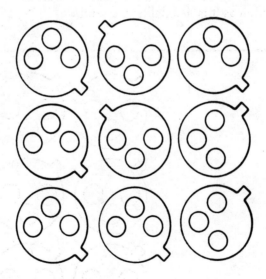

FIGURE 10-10
This arrangement
has added a
second
orientation
results of a cost
factor increase to
1.45.

FIGURE 10-11 A
third orientation
results in a cost
factor increase to
1.85

*FIGURE 10-12 A
random
arrangement. This
arrangement has
more than
doubled the cost
factor to 2.25.*

A little forethought in design and manufacturing of printed circuit boards make a big difference in the cost of the assembly. Designers usually have no direct control over the assembly method or insertion machine used in production, but by choosing the simplest and most feasible component arrangement, this frees the manufacturing engineer to select the most economical method.

Designers also need to be aware of the relationship of the board size, hole sizes, insertable area for the component, and component spacing to the requirements of the automatic insertion machine. If possible, the designer should try to limit the printed circuit board design on component orientation. Also try to keep components with the same orientation grouped together.

Chapter

11

ARTMASTER
TAPE-UP

ARTMASTER TAPE-UP

The artmaster, Figure 11-1, is a tool which is generally prepared at an enlarged scale used to photographically produce the master pattern. It is constructed by accurately placing precision width tapes and pads on a stable based polyester film, such as mylar, to represent conductors on the finished board. The tape widths, pad diameters and other conductor patterns must be accurately calculated to insure that the desired mass of conducting material will be the result on the completed product.

SCALE

The most common artmaster scales are 2/1 and 4/1 although there are some companies that work at 3/1 and 5/1 scales. It must be noted that the two latter scales, 3/1 and 5/1, are not industry standards and should be avoided.

BASE MATERIAL

Artwork base material should be .005 to .007-in. thick stable-based polyester film. This material, is temperature and humidity stable, and provides a smooth nonporous surface to which tape and patterns will adhere best.

TAPE AND PADS

Black crepe tape, pads and patterns provide a material that is easy to work with and the traces can be routed either by the sweeping bend method or by the cut and bend method. The latter is preferred due to the fact that better proficiency in both time and appearance can be accomplished in a shorter learning time. With the black crepe method, a separate layer or sheet must be prepared for each side of the board. This can be accomplished by a two layer method of Figure 11-2 where the first layer has all the pads plus the traces from one side of the board and the second layer has the same pads spotted with the traces from the opposite side.

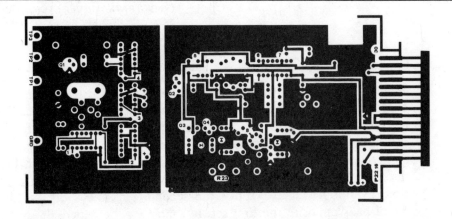

FIGURE 11-1
Artmaster

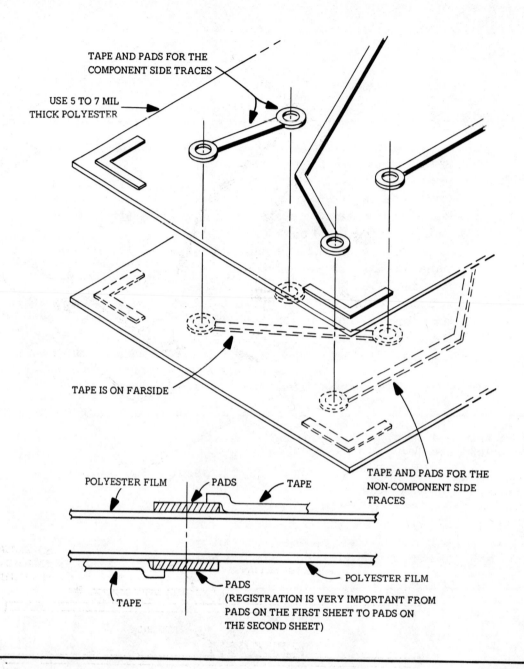

TAPE AND PADS FOR THE
COMPONENT SIDE TRACES

USE 5 TO 7 MIL
THICK POLYESTER

TAPE IS ON FARSIDE

TAPE AND PADS FOR THE
NON-COMPONENT SIDE
TRACES

POLYESTER FILM   PADS   TAPE

POLYESTER FILM

PADS

TAPE

(REGISTRATION IS VERY IMPORTANT FROM
PADS ON THE FIRST SHEET TO PADS ON
THE SECOND SHEET)

FIGURE 11-2
Two Layer
Method

The three layer method shown in Figure 11-3 is essentially the same except one layer is used for a "pad pattern," and then this is overlaid with a sheet for the non-component traces and a different sheet for the component traces. This method saves time by not having to "spot" the second set of pads opposite the first set, but most important, insures perfect registration of all pads from component side to non-component side because the same pad pattern is used for both sides with the respective trace pattern superimposed over it.

The red and blue material method illustrated in Figure 11-4 provides tapes in the same widths as black crepe except they can be taped on one sheet of polyester film with red on one side and blue on the other

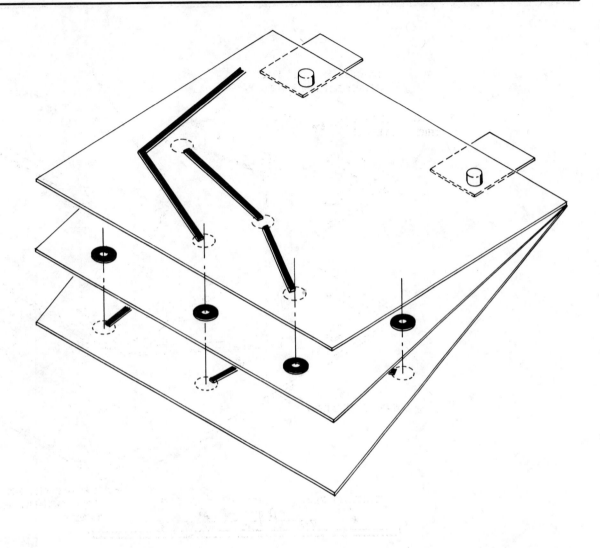

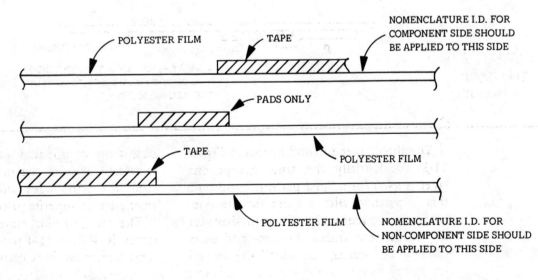

POLYESTER FILM

TAPE

NOMENCLATURE I.D. FOR
COMPONENT SIDE SHOULD
BE APPLIED TO THIS SIDE

PADS ONLY

TAPE

POLYESTER FILM

POLYESTER FILM

NOMENCLATURE I.D. FOR
NON-COMPONENT SIDE SHOULD
BE APPLIED TO THIS SIDE

FIGURE 11-3
Three Layer
Method

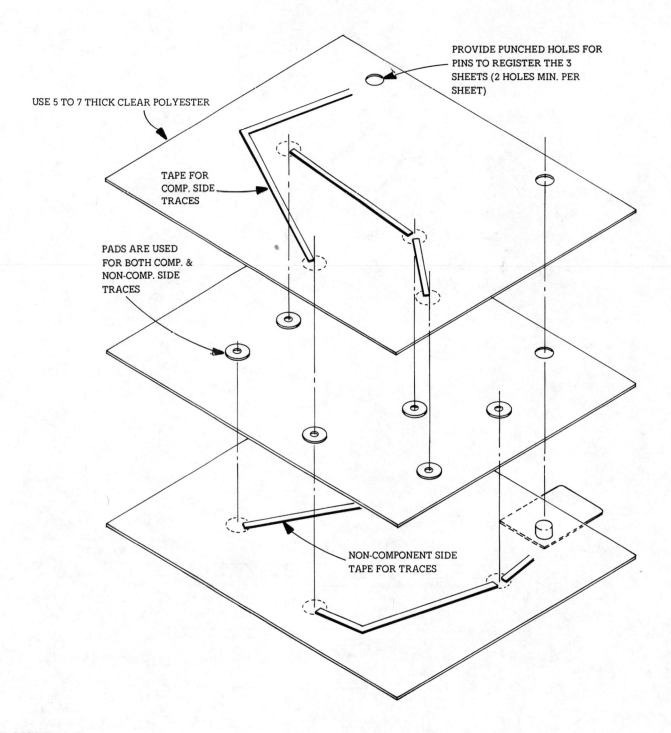

PROVIDE PUNCHED HOLES FOR PINS TO REGISTER THE 3 SHEETS (2 HOLES MIN. PER SHEET)

USE 5 TO 7 THICK CLEAR POLYESTER

TAPE FOR COMP. SIDE TRACES

PADS ARE USED FOR BOTH COMP. & NON-COMP. SIDE TRACES

NON-COMPONENT SIDE TAPE FOR TRACES

FIGURE 11-3a
Three Layer
Method

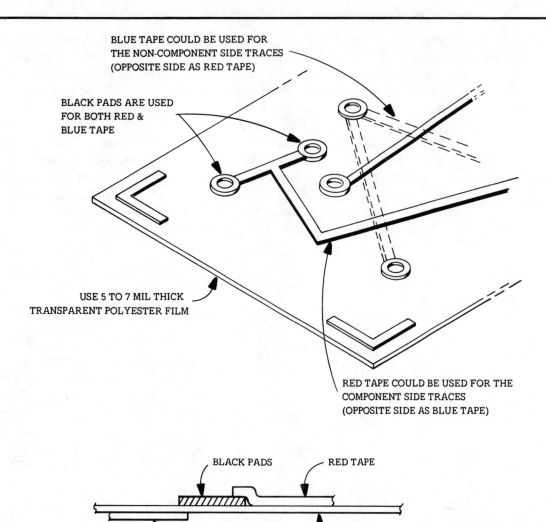

BLUE TAPE COULD BE USED FOR
THE NON-COMPONENT SIDE TRACES
(OPPOSITE SIDE AS RED TAPE)

BLACK PADS ARE USED
FOR BOTH RED &
BLUE TAPE

USE 5 TO 7 MIL THICK
TRANSPARENT POLYESTER FILM

RED TAPE COULD BE USED FOR THE
COMPONENT SIDE TRACES
(OPPOSITE SIDE AS BLUE TAPE)

BLACK PADS   RED TAPE

FIGURE 11-4
One Sheet Red &
Blue Method

BLUE TAPE   POLYESTER FILM

side. The pads would be black crepe placed only on one side and, as in the three layer method, would be used in both the component side and non-component side.

This method allows the photographer, by the use of red and blue filters on his camera, to filter out the blue tape in one case and photograph only the red tape with the black pads for one side of the board. He then changes the filters, repeats the process and photographs only the blue tape with the black pads for the opposite side of the board. The tape-up does not have to be flipped over or moved during this entire process. The end result is absolute registration for two-sided P.C. Boards.

Red and blue tape is not as easy to work with because of its rigid polyvinyl composition. It is more difficult to cut and takes more pain to insure that it will stick to the base polyester film. Red and blue cannot be bent without distortion of the traces; therefore, it has to be cut all the way through and repositioned each time you change direction with a trace or, using the cut and bend method, cut the tape approximately 90 percent through and then bend the remainder to the required degree necessary and burnish down the edges to keep the uncut edge from sticking up.

TAPING STANDARDS Regardless of taping methods or type of material used, the physical act of taping must conform to some basic standards.

Conductor angles should be made at preferred angles of 30, 45 or 90 degrees. Although the traces could be directed at almost any angle, it is important that all traces running parallel be at the same angle for uniformity. The minimum angle that any trace should be placed at is 90 degrees. Angles less than 90 degrees provide a situation during the manufacturing process which could allow etching solution to build up on the inside angle and etch away excess material as illustrated in Figure 11-5.

CONDUCTOR ROUTING

The same problems discussed under "Conductor Angles" also apply to trace routing. If the junction of traces coming off a pad form a pocket, the same over-etching problem can occur as shown in figure 11-6.

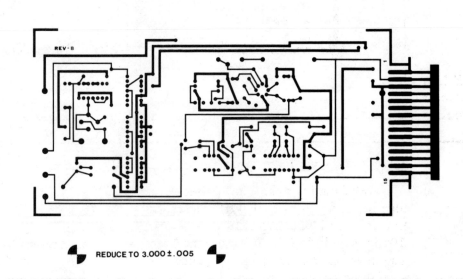

Typical Tape-Up

REDUCE TO 3.000 ± .005

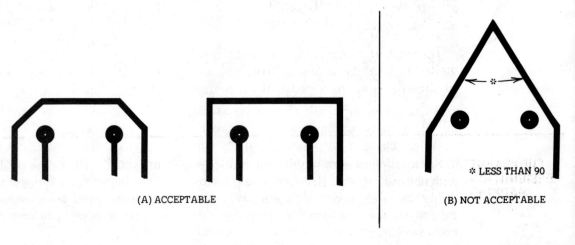

FIGURE 11-5
Conductor Angles

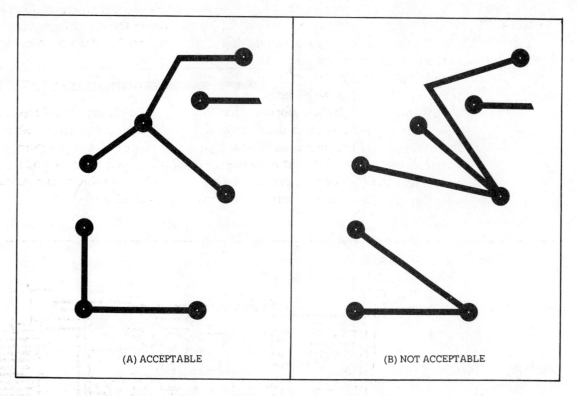

FIGURE 11-6
Conductor
Routing

(A) ACCEPTABLE

(B) NOT ACCEPTABLE

CONDUCTOR SPACING TO BOARD EDGE

Traces should not come any closer to the edge of the board than .050-in. at a scale of 1x1 inch and, if at all possible, at least .100-in. should be left. This gives the board manufacturer the necessary tolerance that is required to shear the board to the size specified. If less than the above-mentioned air gap is left, a portion or all of the trace could get sheared off or shorted out at the next assembly.

If metal or electrically conductive card guides are used, then the gap from the edge of the card guide to the edge of the nearest conductor should be the standard required air gap (.050-in. or greater); see Figure 11-7.

TAPING DON'TS

There should be no overlapping of tape or cutting of pads. Tape has a natural tendency to "creep" or return back to its original shape if it is bent or stretched at all. Even under the most careful conditions, this can be a problem so care must be taken not to create even more difficult situations where tape could distort and cause electrical and manufacturing problems. See Figure 11-8.

COMPONENT DESIGNATION MARKING

Some applications require all reference designations of the electrical components either be etched or silk-screened on the P.C. board for easy identification. This aids technicians and field service repairmen to repair or trouble-shoot boards without the use of an assembly or loading diagram. Boards that have a high failure rate or have to be repaired by persons without proper access to a full documentation package rely on this information.

In cases where such rigid identification is

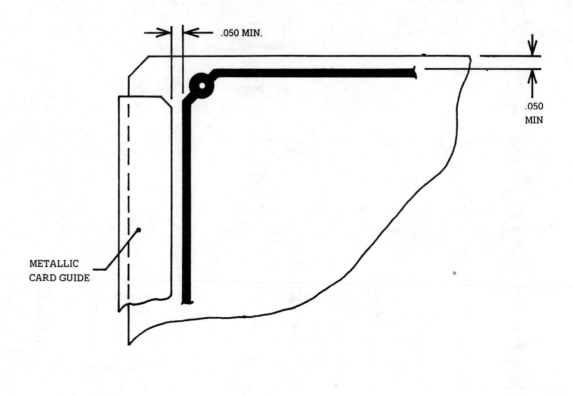

.050 MIN.

.050 MIN

METALLIC
CARD GUIDE

FIGURE 11-7
*Spacing for
Conductive Card
Guides*

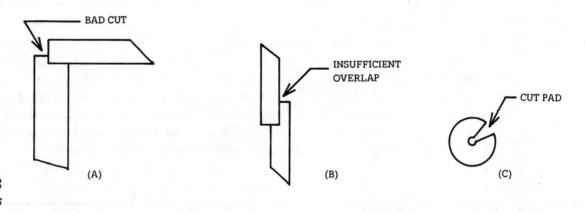

BAD CUT

INSUFFICIENT
OVERLAP

CUT PAD

(A)

(B)

(C)

FIGURE 11-8
Taping Problems

not necessary, it is still important to identify such components as connectors, test points, switches or any component that will require access for calibration or trouble-shooting. If a particular board requires that jumpers be installed to reflect different models or functions, then they should be marked on the board also.

Integrated circuit packages should be identified on the board. The IC's are not generally oriented in any numerical sequence on the schematic. Therefore, in order to relate a reference designation from the schematic to the P.C. board, the integrated circuit (IC) mechanical package must be identified by a reference designation number on the board for quick reference.

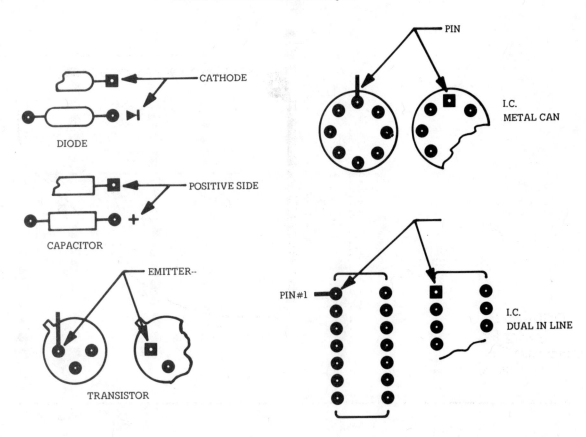

FIGURE 11-9
Board Reference
Designations

It is helpful to identify enough of the contacts on a connector or any other cluster of pins that are pre-assigned a number arrangement. Generally, the first and last pins are enough to establish this sequence; in other cases, the first or last pins in each row might be required. If a particular board uses jumpers to distinguish to electrical difference between models, it is a good idea to identify these.

In general, keep in mind that little effort is required to clarify a patented problem at the design stage, whereas downstream a solution could be costly.

POLARITY AND INDEXING

Components that must be oriented in a fixed direction due to polarity or pin arrangements should be indexed on the board (as in Figure 11-10). This consideration is not only a must for the manufacturing stage of the board, but it is also relied upon by the technician, engineer, field service representative, customer and any other person that would have need to trouble-shoot or follow the flow of the circuit on the P.C. board.

It is very helpful to index various pins on a connector to aid in finding a particular pin number. In addition to identifying the pin number as described in "Board Reference Designations," Figure 11-11, every tenth pin could be indexed. In large connectors, this would allow the technician to

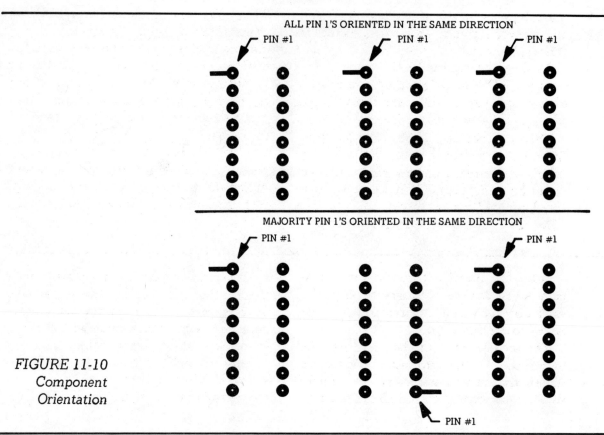

FIGURE 11-10
Component
Orientation

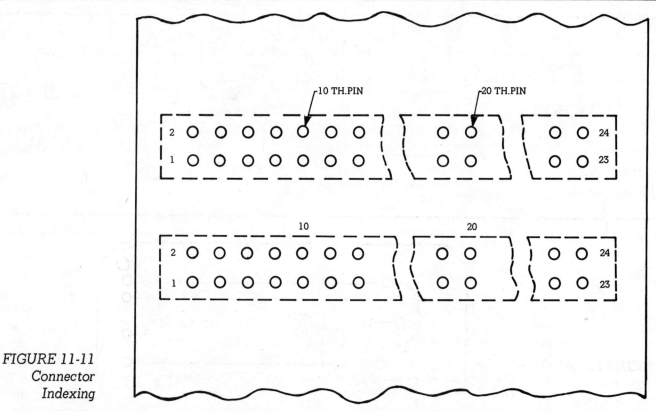

FIGURE 11-11
Connector
Indexing

scan the pins in sets of ten until he found the nearest segment which that particular pin was located.

As shown in Figure 11-12 integrated circuits should be placed on the board so that all are oriented in the same direction in addition to having pin "1" indexed.

This practice aids the technician in finding a particular pin on an integrated circuit without first turning the board over to see how that particular package was oriented, pin "1" top or bottom.

In some dense packaging applications, due to the flow of the circuit and the pin assignments of some integrated circuits (i.e., counters), it is not possible to follow this pin orientation process. The designer should still strive for consistent orientation as much as possible allowing only those packages which won't conform to break the pattern.

In general, any component or pad which could be confusing or oriented improperly during the assembly stage should be identified by polarity marking or an indexing feature.

After the board is taped and is electrically ready for the photography step, the final documentation information must be added to the tape-up.

The revision letter of the board must be identified on the artmaster somewhere within the board parameters. This allows for it to be actually etched on the board to avoid confusion with any previous or later changes that might occur. This is generally done as in Figure 11-13 on the non-component side of the board along with the P.C. board part number, if applicable.

The assembly number of the board should be identified in the same manner on the component side of the board. This gives

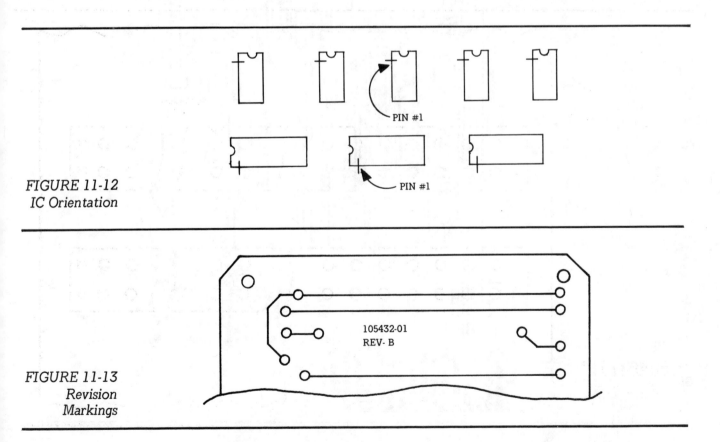

FIGURE 11-12
IC Orientation

FIGURE 11-13
Revision
Markings

quick reference to anyone in finding the proper assembly drawing and any other documentation involved in the manufacturing, procurement or sale of the board. No assembly revision letter should be etched on the board; this information should be added at the actual stage at whatever revision the assembly drawing is at the time the board is assembled.

The master pattern number refers to the artmaster itself and will document the number and revision letter of the finished tool to which the board is made. This number and revision letter is important for traceability purposes in case failure of the final product should result. This identification marking should be outside the pa-rameter of the board as it will not be part of the physical board once it is manufactured, and it should be entered in the documentation system.

The reduction targets and dimensions provide very necessary information to the photographer to aid him in the proper reduction of the artmaster. Targets should be carefully and accurately placed so that they will appear on all copies of the master pattern. Reduction marking should extend along one vertical side and/or along one horizontal side of the tape-up.

Examples of an artwork master containing the master pattern number and reduction targets are shown in Figure 11-14.

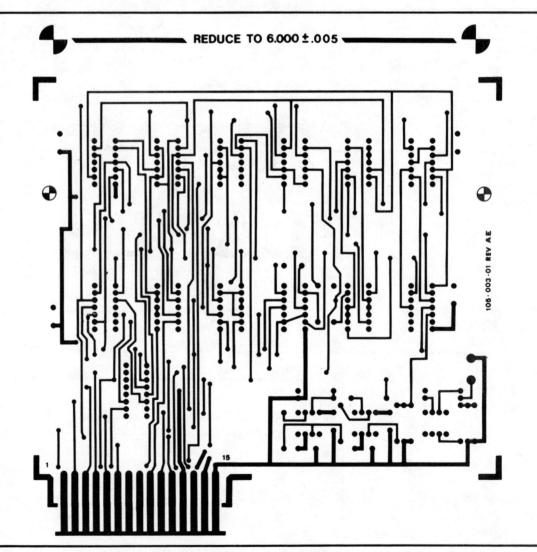

REDUCE TO 6.000 ±.005

105-003-01 REV AE

FIGURE 11-14
Artwork Master
Showing Reduction
Targets

Chapter

12

GROUND PLANES

Ground planes are areas on the P.C. board that have not been consumed by traces or pads and are left with copper that is tied to the ground circuit (See Figure 12-1). The plane is generally on the component side, especially for flow soldering, and is isolated from the other traces and pads. Planes on the component side of the P.C. board are typically a continuous conduc-tive area. Planes on the non-component side of the P.C. board wider than .05-in. should be broken up into a striped or checkered pattern (see Figure 12-2). This will help prevent blistering and warping during the flow soldering operation.

Adequate clearance should be provided around nonfunctional terminating areas in ground planes on external board layers. On

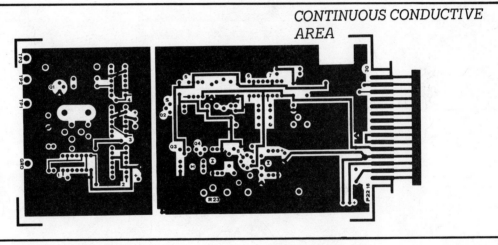

CONTINUOUS CONDUCTIVE AREA

FIGURE 12-1

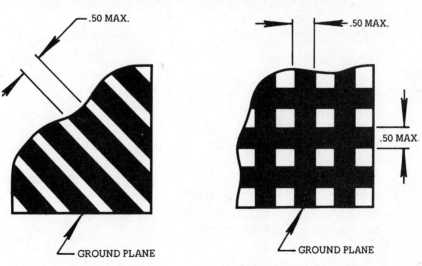

.50 MAX.

.50 MAX.

.50 MAX.

GROUND PLANE

GROUND PLANE

FIGURE 12-2

internal layers of multilayer boards, use of a nonfunctional terminal area is not necessary if a diameter is left clear around the hole. See Figure 12-3.

When a hole terminates in a ground plane and electrical continuity is required, a terminal area should be used. Clearance should be provided between the terminal area and ground plane for two to four connections to preserve circuit continuity. See Figure 12-4. This prevents "heat sinking" of the terminal area during soldering operations; this can result in an inferior solder joint.

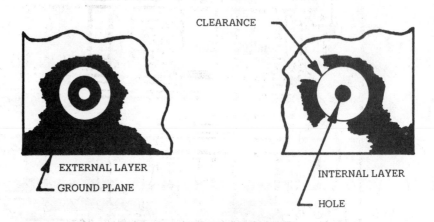

FIGURE 12-3
Nonfunctional
Terminal Area
Such As
Mounting Holes,
Tooling Holes

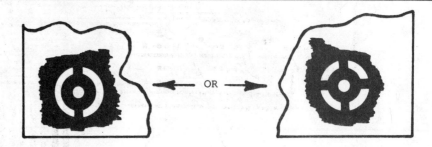

FIGURE 12-4

GROUND PLANE ART MASTERS

Ground should not be connected by means of tape. The ground plane can be transposed onto the photo-master by a photographic process. Care must be taken by the designer during his initial layout to assure one continuous ground plane. After the board is taped, a blue print of the component side of the artmaster can be used to show the photographer the ground plane limitations, and connections to be made. This print shall be sent to the photographers along with the artmaster and will be used to create the ground plane. See Figure 12-5.

NOTES FOR THE PHOTOGRAPHER—(THESE NOTES ARE TO BE PLACED ON OR ACCOMPANY THE BLUE PRINT.)

NOTES:

1. Ground plane side shown only
2. Air gap to be .XXX at 1/1 scale
3. Connect all indicated pads to ground plane
4. Remove all isolated grounds
5. Remove ground plane limitation line from finished neg. and positive

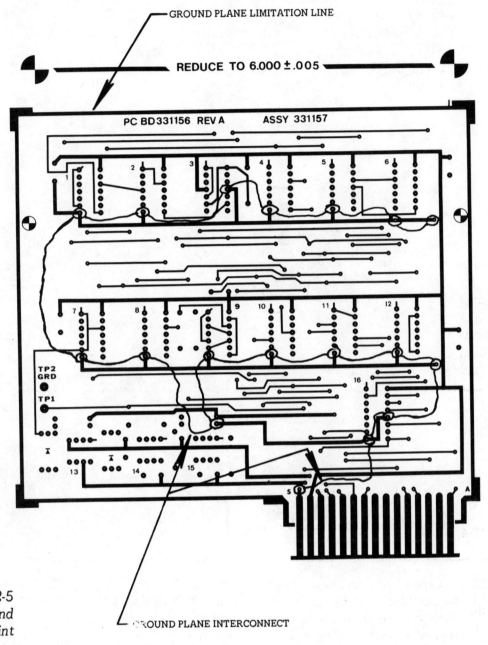

GROUND PLANE LIMITATION LINE

REDUCE TO 6.000 ±.005

PC BD331156 REV A   ASSY 331157

TP2
GRD

TP1

FIGURE 12-5
Typical Ground
Plane Print

GROUND PLANE INTERCONNECT

Chapter

13

FAMILIARIZATION WITH FABRICATION DRAWINGS

DETAIL FABRICATION DRAWING

The detail fabrication drawing of the printed circuit board shall depict the dimensional configuration of the board, size and location of holes, and shall specify the material, process specifications and (if applicable) notes and other information necessary for the fabrication of printed circuit board. Figure 13-1 shows a typical P.C. board detail drawing; detailed considerations are given below.

The detail fabrication drawing should be drawn in the same scale as the film or photomaster (normally). If more than one scale is used, each scale shall be clearly identified.

All dimensions needed to fabricate the P.C. board should be shown with the exception of those features located by the film or photomaster, such as pads, traces, connector fingers, etc. Dimensions for board configuration should be referenced from the tooling holes or register marks etched on the printed circuit board. All holes, cutouts, and the board outline shall be dimensioned from these points.

The detail fabrication drawing should show the non-component side of the P.C. board. One reason is because the manufacturer would like to view the side of the board that is drilled. Another reason is because of the burr left on the opposite side of drilling after the drill passes through the P.C. board.

The purpose of having the burr on the component side of the P.C. board is because widespread use of wave or flow soldering. This process requires that the side passing through the wave of solder be smooth, and the non-component side must be the side that passes through or over the wave of solder.

Manufacturing information, including plating and process specifications, shall be noted on the detail fabrication drawing (See examples below). Figure 13-2 shows a number of examples.

1. Hole sizes are after plating.
2. Circuit side of card shown.
3. Printed circuit board must conform to XXXX specification (See plating specifications below).
4. Printed circuit per photomaster XXXX, Revision X.
5. Hole diameter tolerance XXX $\pm^{.005}_{.002}$

The hole schedule chart appears on the face of the detail drawing and will give the symbol used to identify each hole called out. It contains a description of each hole size and tolerance, and if necessary, the quantity of each type or size used.

Listed below are most of the basic plating specifications requirements that must be provided to the P.C. board manufacturer. These specifications will not conform to all companies' standards; therefore, use these specs where applicable.

1. *Base Laminate:* Base material shall be laminated epoxy glass type G10, .06 ±.002 thick.

2. *Conductor:* Conductor material on double-sided (plated through) board shall be 1 oz. or 2 oz. copper minimum before plating.

3. *Solder Plating:* The tin lead alloy plating shall contain 40% ±5% lead and 60%

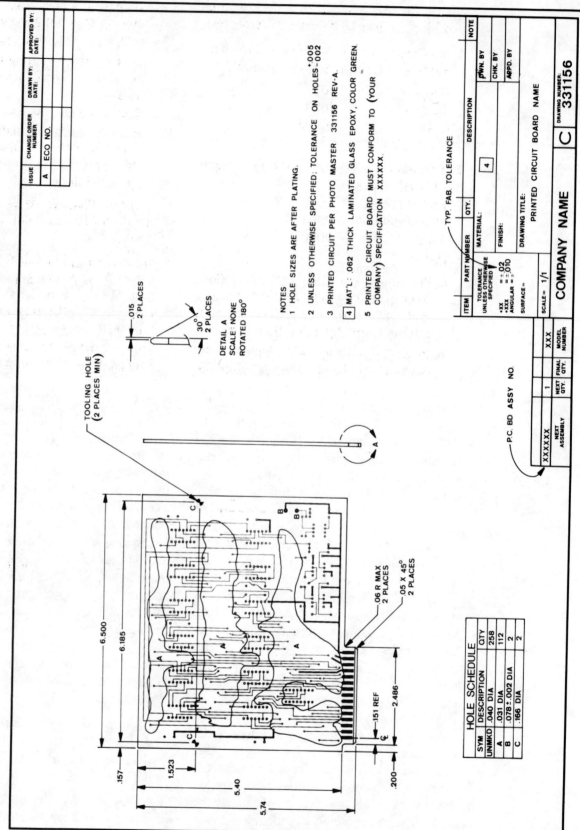

FIGURE 13-1
Typical Assembly
Drawing

±5% tin. All solder-plated areas shall be subject to hot oil solder reflow process.

4. *Minimum Plating Thickness on Trace Surface and Through Holes* (inches):

Copper	.001
Tin-lead	.0003
Gold	.00005
Nickel-gold	.003

5. *Minimum Plating Thickness for Fingers* (inches):

Nickel-gold	.0003
Nickel-rhodium	.0003
Gold	.00005

6. *Conductor Defects:*

   a. Pin holes, nicks, and scratches: Conductor defects such as pin holes and nicks which do not reduce the conductor width by more than ±.002-in.

   b. Plating overhang: The plated resist material overhang remaining after the copper foil has been removed by etching shall not exceed .005-in.

   c. Undercut: The reduction of conductor caused by etching under the edge of plating resist shall not exceed .005-in.

   d. Excess conductor material: Isolated spots of conductor material no greater than .015-in. in diameter are acceptable providing spacing requirements are not violated.

7. *Warpage:* Warpage or twist of a printed circuit board shall not exceed .005-in. per inch.

8. *Solderability:* The solder coating shall be adherent and non-granular in appearance. The base material shall not show evidence of blistering or delamination, nor shall conductors or terminal areas show evidence of separating from the base laminate after dip soldering.

Hole Schedule		
Symbol	Description	Qty.
Unmarked	.038 Dia.	—
A	.048 Dia.	59
B	.187 Dia.	7

TABLE 13-1

NOTES UNLESS OTHERWISE SPECIFIED:

1. Hole sizes are after plating.
2. Circuit side of card shown.
3. Printed circuit board must conform to **XXX** specification.
4. Printed circuit per photo master.
5. Hole diameter tolerance = +.005
   −.002

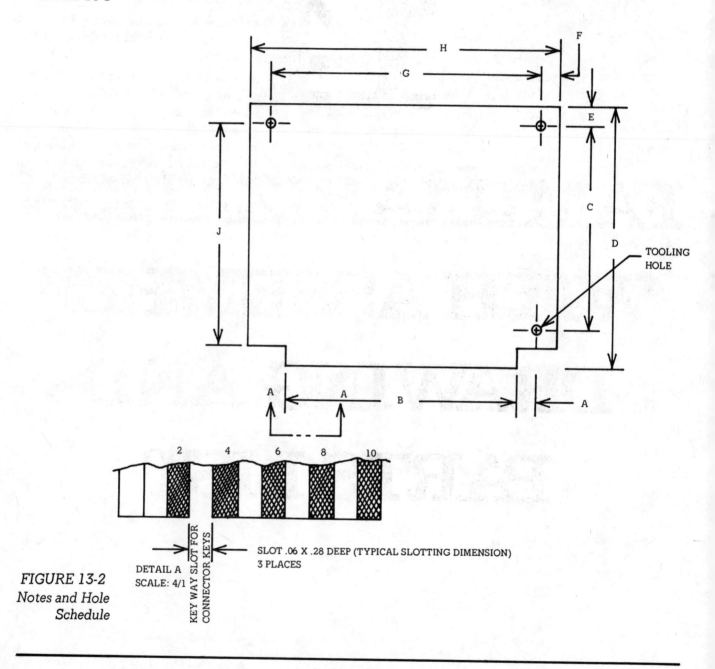

FIGURE 13-2
Notes and Hole Schedule

Chapter

14

FAMILIARIZATION WITH ASSEMBLY DRAWING AND PARTS LIST

The printed circuit assembly drawing should meet the normal requirements of an assembly drawing. It should depict the P.C. board components, reference designation markings, assembly and test specs, and also include a list of material which contains all part information needed to order the parts. A typical assembly drawing is shown in Figure 14-1; detailed considerations are given below.

SCALE

The assembly drawing is normally drawn in the same scale as the artwork or tape-up. If more than one scale is used, each scale shall be clearly identified.

VIEW

The assembly drawing shall be drawn as viewed from the component side. Also a side view shall be shown to indicate the maximum component height relative to the board. Enlarged views or sections may be used if needed for clarification.

SYMBOLS & REFERENCE DESIGNATIONS

Symbols and reference designations should be shown per the applicable schematic diagram. Abbreviations, if used, shall be per MIL-STD-12C or applicable company standards. Reference designations should also be used to identify all electrical components from the assembly drawing back to the schematic and parts list, (Figure 14-2).

MOUNTING

Methods for mounting the components, such as riveting, soldering, brackets, etc., shall be noted.

JUMPERS

If wire terminations are used for circuit interconnections and are not etched or marked on the P.C. board, the wire terminations shall be identified as jumper wires and shown on the assembly drawing.

ORIENTATION & INDEXING

All transistor tabs should be shown unless it is an epoxy-type transistor, which will be indicated by the flat side. TO-18 and TO-5 case pins 8 or 10 should be marked. For dual-in-line cases, pin 1 should be marked. All polarized capacitors (plus side) and all diodes (cathode end) should also be marked.

NOTES

Sample P.C. assembly drawing notes, as applicable, are listed below.

1. Reference electrical schematic diagram **XXXXXXX**.

2. Assemble and solder per **XXXX** spec (or **XXXXX** standard practice).

3. Observe polarity of capacitors, diodes, etc.

4. Mark assembly number and revision letter (per applicable company standard).

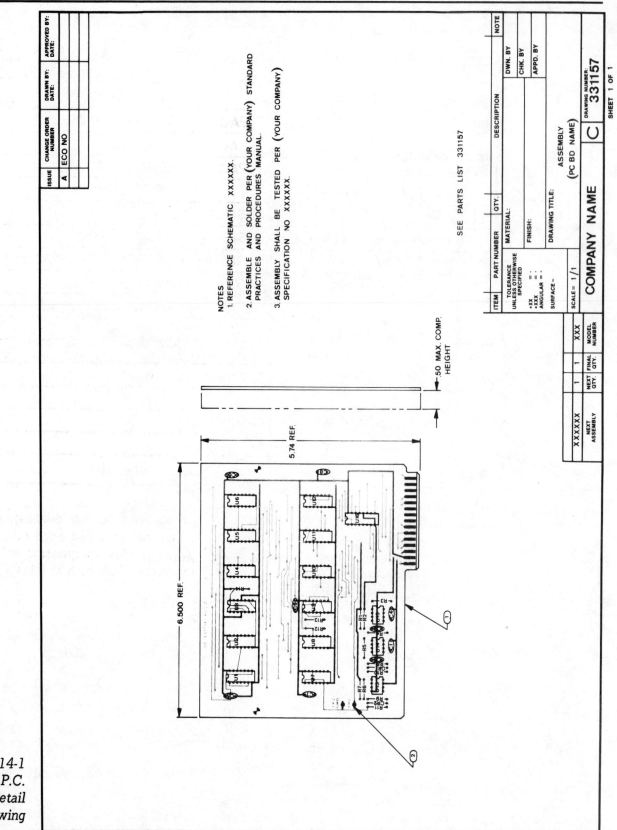

FIGURE 14-1
Typical P.C.
Board Detail
Drawing

REF DES	ITEM NO.	MANUFACTURERS PART NUMBER	DESCRIPTION	TOTAL QTY
ASSEMBLY NAME: POWER SUPPLY			PARTS LIST	
ASSEMBLY NUMBER: 331578				
C1		CKO5	CAPACITOR, CERAMIC 0.1 UF, 10V	3
C2		CKO5	CAPACITOR, CERAMIC 0.1 UF, 10V	-
C3		CKO5	CAPACITOR, CERAMIC 0.1 UF, 10V	-
R1		89PR5K	RESISTOR, VARIABLE 5K	1
R2		JANRCRO7	RESISTOR, CARBON 560, 1/4W, 5%	2
R3		JANRCRO7	RESISTOR, CARBON 4 7K, 1/4W, 5%	1
R4		89PR10K	RESISTOR, VARIABLE 10K	1
R5		JANRCRO7	RESISTOR, CARBON 560, 1/4W, 5%	-
Q1		2N3210	TRANSISTOR NPN	2
Q2		2N3210	TRANSISTOR NPN	-
U1		LM741	OP-AMP	2
U2		LM741	OP-AMP	-

FIGURE 14-2
Parts List

5. Board to be conformal coated in accordance with XXXX MIL Spec. Test points and adjustable components shall be masked during coating.

6. Electrical reference designations are for reference only and need not appear on the parts or components unless otherwise specified, such as R1, C1, CR1, etc.

Chapter

15

SILKSCREEN DRAWINGS AND ARTMASTERS

The silkscreen drawing and artmaster provide a tool from which silkscreens, stamps, stencils or other marking mediums are fabricated for marking the printed circuit board with reference markings prior to assembly of the components.

SILKSCREEN ARTMASTER

The artmaster seen in Figure 15-1 should have sharp definition and high contrast because it is reproduced by a photographic process.

The silkscreen artmaster should be a transparent, stable material either with black self-sticking printed circuit tape, black matte characters having a heat resistant, pressure sensitive adhesive backing or black ink lettering with a "Leroy" or similar type pen. The tape and pre-printed characters are preferred because of their well defined lines and uniform contrast.

Ragged edges, splits on the line work or characters, and pinholes should be avoided in order to reduce the amount of retouching.

The artmaster should be made to the same scale as the printed circuit artmaster.

The silkscreen artmaster is an undimensioned master. The artmaster should show the accurately scaled distance between two target points in the horizontal or vertical planes; both horizontal and vertical are not necessary, but may be used.

Tooling holes or fabrication lines for the artmaster should be located on the artmaster to correspond with those on the printed circuit artmaster.

All markings should be taken from the schematic or bill of materials (reference designations) of the printed circuit board. They should be located to cause no identification confusion.

SILKSCREEN DRAWING

The silkscreen drawing is an undimensioned drawing used primarily to denote color of silkscreen and special instructions, Figure 15-2.

The silkscreen drawing should be made to the same scale as the artmaster or reduced to fit the drawing size. If the artmaster scale is too large, it should be drawn as reviewed from the component side of the printed circuit board.

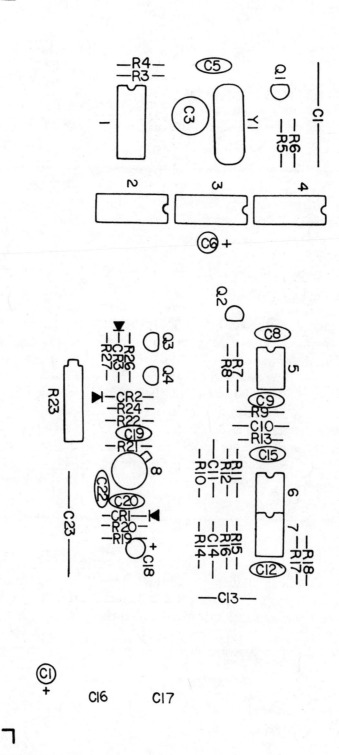

FIGURE 15-1
Artmaster

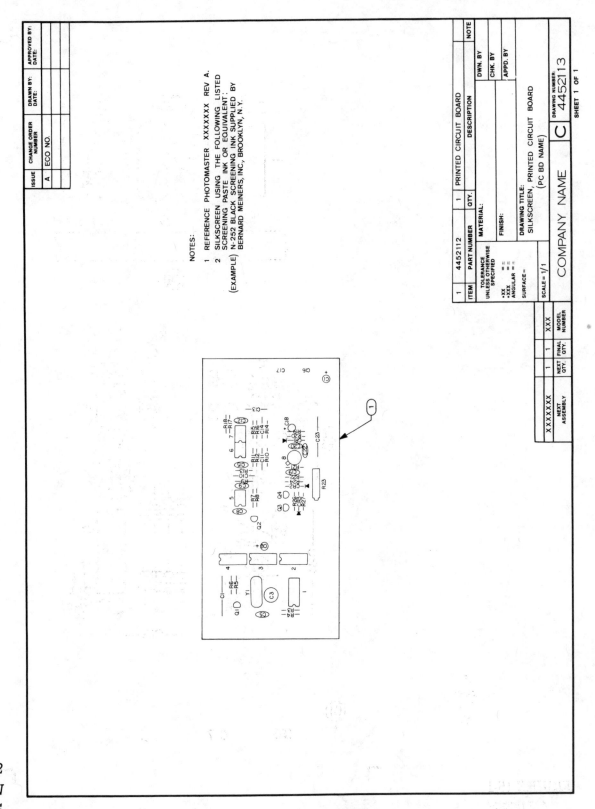

FIGURE 15-2
SILKSCREEN
DRAWING

Chapter

16

MANUFACTURING PROCESS OF P.C. BOARDS

Today, the printed circuit board market is over $1 Billion and growing. Most of that is being spent on a manufacturing technique called "subtractive process." This essentially is a 30-year old technology summarized in Table 16-1. There is now a new technology called "additive process," summarized in Table 16-2. Today there is a constant pressure throughout the entire electronics industry to provide more compact and denser P.C. boards. This pressure has brought about the use of solder masks which will be discussed further in this chapter.

The basic sequence for manufacturing P.C. boards by the conventional or subtractive process:

Starting with panels of copper clad base material to be consistent, holes are fabricated by drilling or piercing. The panels are sensitized and given an electroless copper flash to make the holes conductive for electroplating. A plating resist mask is applied by screening or photoprinting and copper is pattern plated with the minimum thickness in the holes, usually at least .001-in. A second metal is plated over the copper to act as an etch resist and to provide corrosion protection for the finished circuit. The screened or photoprinted mask is stripped, the background copper is etched and a solder mask may be applied if specified by the end-user.

The basic sequence for manufacturing P.C. boards by the additive process:

TABLE 16-1

A.	Copper clad base material.
B.	Drill or pierce holes.
C.	Sensitize holes.
D.	Electroless copper flash.
E.	Print reverse pattern mask.
F.	Electroplate copper.
G.	Electroplate etch resist metal.
H.	Strip Mask.
I.	Etch foil copper.
J.	Apply solder mask (optional).

TABLE 16-2

A.	Adhesive coated unclad laminate.
B.	Drill or pierce holes.
C.	Print reverse pattern mask.
D.	Activate.
E.	Electroless copper deposition
F.	Strip Mask (optional).
G.	Apply solder mask (optional).
H.	Apply protective overcoat.

The process begins with panels of catalytic base material coated with a thin layer of catalytic adhesive. The base material can be any type normally used for conventional circuits and the adhesive can be applied either by the laminate supplier or by the printed circuit manufacturer. After hole formation by drilling or piercing, a reverse pattern is applied by screening or photo-printing. A chemical activation cycle prepares the adhesive for copper deposition to achieve bond strengths averaging 12 to 14

pounds per inch. When the panels are placed in the electroless copper bath, copper autocatalytically deposits to the required thickness. This thickness can range from copper foil equivalent of 1/4 to 2 ounces. If the plating resist is not a permanent epoxy mask, a stripping operation follows and a solder mask is applied to one or two sides if required. To insure future solderability and protect against oxidation, the copper is protected with an inexpensive, organic resin coating.

SOLDER MASK

Solder masking is a screened on coat of epoxy resin, covering all areas of the P.C. board except pads which require soldering. Clearance around these pads would typically be .010-in.

With the current industry trend toward higher density boards with tighter line widths and spacing, solder masks are increasingly being used to eliminate bridging

between adjacent conductors during wave soldering. When applied to a conventional circuits with the usual tin-lead overplate, these masks have a tendency to chip and peel when the overplate reflows.

NOTE: Bridging is excess solder build up and shorts out adjacent conductors

---

BOARD CHARACTERISTICS AFFECTING SOLDERABILITY

There are four characteristics of a P.C. board which are major factors in its solderability and rejects or rework after the final assembly is wave-soldered. These are:

A. Characteristics of the metal plating.
B. Conductor overhang and undercut.
C. Hole wall plating.
D. Solder masks.

In each of these four areas, there are differences between boards manufactured by conventional subtractive process and the additive process which can affect the solderability and acceptability of the final assembly. Inter-relationship of these variables plus the additional factors involved in the soldering operation such as speed over the wave, solder temperature, tinlead ratio, type of flux and methods of application,

angle of the board through the wave, component lead to hole clearance, etc., make it very difficult to quantify the range of effects each of these characteristics can have on the final soldering operation.

During wave soldering, this can cause bridging in spite of the mask which will increase inspection time and rework. Overplates other than tin-lead can alleviate this condition but their higher cost or poorer solderability may result in only substituting one additional cost problem for another.

In the fully additive process, the solder mask is applied directly to the copper rather than an overplate. Since there is no deformation of the copper, excellent adhesion is maintained during wave soldering and no premium for a special overplate is required.

Chapter

17

DESIGN REFERENCE MATERIALS

TERMS APPLICABLE TO PRINTED CIRCUIT BOARDS

1. **AIR GAP:** The non-conductive air space between traces, pads, conductive matter, or any combination thereof.

2. **ANALOG CIRCUIT:** A circuit comprised mostly of discrete components (i.e., resistors, capacitors, transistors) which produces data represented by physical variables such as voltage, resistance, rotation, etc.

3. **ANNULAR RING:** The width of the conductor surrounding a hole through a Printed Circuit Pad.

4. **ARTWORK:** An accurately scaled configuration used to produce a Master Pattern. Generally prepared at an enlarged scale using various width tapes and special shapes to represent conductors.

5. **AWG:** American Wire Gage. A method of specifying wire diameter. The higher the number, the smaller the diameter.

6. **AXIAL LEADS:** Leads coming out the ends and along the axis of a resistor, capacitor, or other axial part, rather than out the side.

7. **BRIDGING:** A condition that generally happens during the wave soldering operation where excess solder builds up and shorts out adjacent conductors.

8. **BUS:** A heavy trace or conductive metal strip on the Printed Circuit Board used to distribute voltage, grounds, etc., to smaller branch traces.

9. **BYPASS CAPACITOR:** A capacitor used for providing a comparatively low impedance A-C path around a circuit element.

10. **CONFORMAL COAT:** A coating that is generally sprayed, dipped, or brushed on to provide the completed Printed Circuit Board protection from fungus, moisture and debris.

11. **CONNECTOR TONGUE:** A protrusion of the Printed Circuit Board edge that is manufactured to a configuration to mate with a receptacle that provides electrical and/or mechanical junction between the Printed Circuit Board and other circuitry.

12. **DIGITAL CIRCUIT:** A circuit comprised of mostly integrated circuits which operates like a switch (i.e., it is either "ON" or "OFF").

13. **DISCRETE COMPONENT:** A component which has been fabricated prior to its installation (i.e., resistors, capacitors, diodes and transistors).

14. **FEED-THRU**: A plated-thru hole in a Printed Circuit Board that is used to provide electrical connection between a trace on one side of the Printed Circuit Board to a trace on the other side. Since it is not used to mount component leads, it is generally a small hole and pad diameter.

15. **FLOW SOLDERING**: Also called wave soldering. A method of soldering Printed Circuit Boards by moving them over a flowing wave of molten solder in a solder bath.

16. **GLASS EPOXY**: A material used to fabricate Printed Circuit Boards. The base material (fiberglass) is impreginated with an epoxy filler which then must have copper laminated to its outer surface to form the material required to manufacture Printed Circuit Boards.

17. **GRID**: A two-dimensional network consisting of a set of equally spaced parallel lines superimposed upon another set of equally spaced parallel lines so that the lines of one set are perpendicular to the lines of the other.

18. **GROUND PLANE**: A condition where all unused areas (areas not consumed by traces or pads) of the Printed Circuit Board are left unetched and tied to the ground circuit throughout the board.

19. **MASTER PATTERN**: An accurately scaled pattern which is used to produce the Printed Circuit within the accuracy specified in the Master Drawing.

20. **MOTHER BOARD**: Also called Back Plane, or Matrix Board. A relatively large Printed Circuit Board on which modules, connectors, sub-assemblies or other Printed Circuit Boards are mounted and inter-connections made by means of traces on the board.

21. **PLATING**: A uniform coating of conductive material upon the base metal of the Printed Circuit Board

22. **RADIAL LEAD**: A lead extending out the side of a component, rather than from the end.

23. **REGISTRATION**: The alignment of a pad on one side of the Printed Circuit Board (or layers of a multi-layer board) to its mating pad on the opposite side.

24. **TOOLING HOLE**: Also called Fabrication Hole, Pilot Hole, or Manufacturing Hole.

RESISTOR AND CAPACITOR STANDARD COLOR CODE

STANDARD COLOR CODE FOR RESISTORS AND CAPACITORS

The standard color code provides the necessary information required to properly identify color coded resistors and capacitors. Refer to the color code for numerical values and the number of zeros (or multiplier) assigned to the colors used. A fourth color band on resistors determines the tolerance rating. Absence of the fourth band indicates a 20% tolerance rating.
(REF MIL-STD-221)

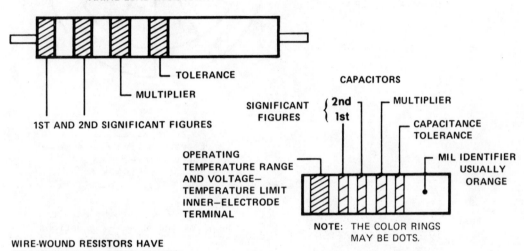

AXIAL LEAD RESISTOR

TOLERANCE

MULTIPLIER

1ST AND 2ND SIGNIFICANT FIGURES

CAPACITORS

SIGNIFICANT FIGURES { 2nd 1st }

MULTIPLIER

CAPACITANCE TOLERANCE

MIL IDENTIFIER USUALLY ORANGE

OPERATING TEMPERATURE RANGE AND VOLTAGE— TEMPERATURE LIMIT INNER—ELECTRODE TERMINAL

NOTE: THE COLOR RINGS MAY BE DOTS.

WIRE-WOUND RESISTORS HAVE
FIRST DIGIT BAND DOUBLE WIDTH

COLOR CODE

COLOR	FIRST FIGURE	SECOND FIGURE	MULTIPLIER	TOLERANCE	
				%	LTR
BLACK	0	0	1		
BROWN	1	1	10		
RED	2	2	100	$\pm$ 2%	G
ORANGE	3	3	1,000		
YELLOW	4	4	10,000		
GREEN	5	5	100,000		
BLUE	6	6	1,000,000		
PURPLE (VIOLET)	7	7			
GRAY	8	8			
WHITE	9	9			
SILVER			0.01	$\pm$ 10%	K
GOLD			0.1	$\pm$ 5%	J
				$\pm$ 20%	M
				$\pm$ 1%	F

OHM'S LAW EQUATIONS

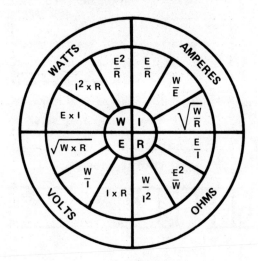

```
W = Power in Watts
E = Electro-Motive Force in Volts
I = Current in Amperes
R = Resistance in Ohms
```

Joule's Law, W = E x I, combined with
Ohm's Law gives the above 12 equations.

CONVERSION OF ELECTRICAL COMPONENT VALUES

CAPACITORS
1,000,000 Microfarads (UF) = 1 Farad
1,000,000 Picofarads (PF) = 1 Microfarad (UF)

RESISTORS
1,000 ohms   = 1 k
1,000,000 ohms = 1 Megohm (Meg)

VOLTS & AMPERES	
1000 Millivolts = 1 Volt	1000 Milliamps = Amp
1000 Microvolts = 1 Millivolt	1000 Microamps = 1 Milliamp

INDUCTANCE
1000 Millihenries = 1 Henry
1000 Microhenries = 1 Millihenry

WIRE CURRENT CAPABILITIES CHART

AWG	FUSING CURRENT (AMPS)	NORMAL LOAD (AMPS)
26	20	0.6
24	29	1.0
22	41	1.6
20	58	2.5
18	83	4.0
16	117	6.0
14	166	15.0
12	235	20.0

1. THE FUSING CURRENT is the current at which the wire will melt.

2. THE NORMAL LOAD (wire rating) is based on 400 circular mils per ampere.

3. Stranded wire specifications allow strands to run from 7 to 19 strands but manufacturers usually use 7 or 19.

How To Use This Chart: Locate the conductor's desired AWG size on the chart and trace it vertically. The number and size of strands needed to make the stranded conductor will be indicated by the horizontal line (strand number) and diagonal line (strand size) respectively.

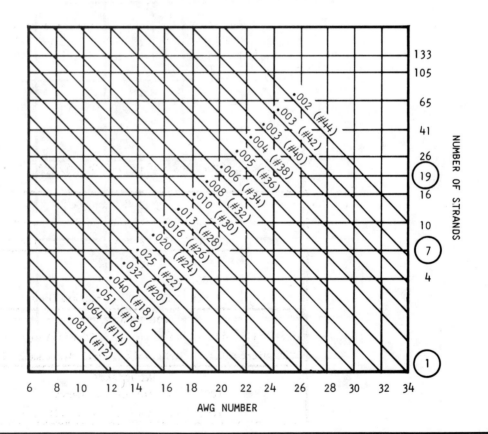

SOLID BARE WIRE GAGE DIAMETERS
AND PRINTED CIRCUIT DRILL SIZES

AMER WIRE GAGE (AWG)	NOM DIA	MM DIA	AREA CIRCULAR MILLS (sq. in.)	OHMS PER 1000 FT at 20°C	FEET PER POUND	PC BOARD HOLE DIA
36	.005	.127	25.0	415.	13,210.	.016 (#78)
35	.0056	.142	31.5	331.	10,481.	.016 (#78)
34	.006	.152	39.8	261.	8,310.	.016 (#78)
33	.007	.178	50.1	206.	6,591.	.016 (#78)
32	.008	.208	63.2	162.	5,227.	.016 (#78)
31	.009	.228	79.7	131.	4,145.	.016 (#78)
30	.010	.254	101.0	104.	3,287.	.016 (#78)
29	.011	.280	127.0	81.2	2,607.	.016 (#78)
28	.013	.330	160.0	65.3	2,067.	.016 (#78)
27	.014	.356	202.0	51.4	1,639.	.026 (#71)
26	.016	.406	254.0	41.0	1,300.	.026 (#71)
25	.018	.457	320.0	32.4	1,031.	.026 (#71)
24	.020	.508	404.0	25.7	817.7	.031 (#68)
23	.023	.584	509.0	20.3	648.4	.031 (#68)
22	.025	.635	642.0	16.2	514.2	.031 (#68)
21	.028	.711	810.0	12.8	407.8	.040 (#60)
20	.032	.813	1,020.0	10.1	323.4	.040 (#60)
19	.036	.914	1,290.0	8.04	256.5	.052 (#55)
18	.040	1.016	1,620.0	6.38	203.4	.052 (#55)
17	.045	1.143	2,050.0	5.04	161.3	.052 (#55)
16	.050	1.270	2,580.0	4.01	127.9	
15	.057	1.448	3,260.0	3.18	101.4	
14	.064	1.626	4,110.0	2.52	80.44	
13	.072	1.829	5,180.0	2.00	63.80	
12	.081	2.057	6,530.0	1.59	50.59	
11	.090	2.286	8,230.0	1.26	40.12	
10	.102	2.590	10,400.0	.999	31.82	
9	.114	2.896	13,100.0	.792	25.23	
8	.128	3.251	16,500.0	.628	20.01	
7	.144	3.658	20,800.0			
6	.162	4.115	26,300.0			
5	.182	4.623	33,100.0			
4	.204	5.182	41,700.0			
3	.229	5.817	52,600.0			
2	.258	6.553	66,400.0			
1	.289	7.340	83,700.0			
0	.325	8.255	106,000.0			

NOTE: PC Board Hole Diameters are for manual insertion and NOT plated through holes.

DRILL SIZES—DECIMAL AND METRIC EQUIVALENTS

SIZE	DECIMAL	MM		SIZE	DECIMAL	MM
85	.011	.2794		41	.096	2.4384
84	.0115	.2921		40	.098	2.4892
83	.012	.3048		39	.0995	2.5273
82	.0125	.3175		38	.1015	2.5780
81	.013	.3302		37	.104	2.6415
80	.0135	.3429		36	.1065	2.7050
79	.0145	.3683		7/64	.1094	2.7787
1/64	.0156	.3962		35	.110	2.7939
78	.016	.4064		34	.111	2.8193
77	.018	.4572		33	.113	2.8701
76	.020	.5080		32	.116	2.9463
75	.021	.5334		31	.120	3.0480
74	.0225	.5715		1/8	.125	3.1749
73	.024	.6096		30	.1285	3.2638
72	.025	.6350		29	.136	3.4543
71	.026	.6604		28	.1405	3.5686
70	.028	.7112		9/64	.1406	3.5712
69	.0292	.7417		27	.144	3.6575
68	.031	.7874		26	.147	3.7337
1/32	.0312	.7925		25	.1495	3.7972
67	.032	.8128		24	.152	3.8607
66	.033	.8382		23	.154	3.9115
65	.035	.8890		5/32	.1562	3.9674
64	.036	.9144		22	.157	3.9877
63	.037	.9398		21	.159	4.0385
62	.038	.9652		20	.161	4.0893
61	.039	.9906		19	.166	4.2163
60	.040	1.0160		18	.1695	4.3052
59	.041	1.0414		11/64	.1719	4.3662
58	.042	1.0668		17	.173	4.3941
57	.043	1.0922		16	.177	4.4957
56	.0465	1.1811		15	.180	4.5719
3/64	.0469	1.1912		14	.182	4.6227
55	.052	1.3208		13	.185	4.6989
54	.055	1.3970		3/16	.1875	4.7624
53	.0595	1.5113		12	.189	4.8005
1/16	.0625	1.5875		11	.191	4.8513
52	.0635	1.6129		10	.1935	4.9148
51	.067	1.7018		9	.196	4.9783
50	.070	1.7780		8	.199	5.0545
49	.073	1.8542		7	.201	5.1053
48	.076	1.9304		13/64	.2031	5.1586
5/64	.0781	1.9837		6	.204	5.1815
47	.0785	1.9939		5	.2055	5.2196
46	.081	2.0574		4	.209	5.3085
45	.082	2.0828		3	.213	5.4101
44	.086	2.1844		7/32	.2188	5.5574
43	.089	2.2606		2	.221	5.6133
42	.0935	2.3749		1	.228	5.7911
3/32	.0938	2.3825				

DRILL SIZES—DECIMAL AND METRIC EQUIVALENTS

(Continued)

SIZE	DECIMAL	MM
A	.234	5.943
15/64	.2344	5.954
B	.238	6.045
C	.242	6.147
D	.246	6.248
E & 1/4	.250	6.350
F	.257	6.528
G	.261	6.629
17/64	.2656	6.746
H	.266	6.756
I	.272	6.909
J	.277	7.036
K	.281	7.137
9/32	.2812	7.142
L	.290	7.366
M	.295	7.493
19/64	.2969	7.541
N	.302	7.671
5/16	.3125	7.937
O	.316	8.026
P	.323	8.204
21/64	.3281	8.334
Q	.332	8.433
R	.339	8.610
11/32	.3438	8.732
S	.348	8.839
T	.358	9.093
23/64	.3594	9.129
U	.368	9.347
3/8	.375	9.525
V	.377	9.576
W	.386	9.804
25/64	.3906	9.921
X	.397	10.084
Y	.404	10.261
13/32	.4062	10.317
Z	.413	10.490

SIZE	DECIMAL	MM
27/64	.4219	10.716
7/16	.4375	11.112
29/64	.4531	11.509
15/32	.4688	11.907
31/64	.4844	12.304
1/2	.5000	12.700
33/64	.5156	13.096
17/32	.5312	13.492
35/64	.5469	13.891
9/16	.5625	14.287
37/64	.5781	14.683
19/32	.5938	15.082
39/64	.6094	15.478
5/8	.625	15.875
41/64	.6406	16.271
21/32	.6562	16.667
43/64	.6719	17.066
11/16	.6875	17.462
45/64	.7031	17.858
23/32	.7188	18.257
47/64	.7344	18.653
3/4	.750	19.050
49/64	.7656	19.446
25/32	.7812	19.842
51/64	.7969	20.241
13/16	.8125	20.637
53/64	.8281	21.033
27/32	.8438	21.432
55/64	.8594	21.828
7/8	.875	22.225
57/64	.8906	22.621
29/32	.9062	23.017
59/64	.9219	23.416
15/16	.9375	23.812
61/64	.9531	24.208
31/32	.9688	24.607
63/64	.9844	25.003
1	1.000	25.400

NOTES: METRIC EQUIVALENTS ARE BASED UPON 1 INCH = 25.3995mm.

TO FIND CENTIMETERS, DIVIDE MILLIMETERS BY 10.

DECADE TABLE

VALUE		PREFIX	SYMBOL	EXAMPLE
1 000 000 000 000	$= 10^{12}$	tera	T	$THz = 10^{12} Hz$
1 000 000 000	$= 10^{9}$	giga	G	$GHz = 10^{9} Hz$
1 000 000	$= 10^{6}$	mega	M	$MHz = 10^{6} Hz$
1 000	$= 10^{3}$	kilo	k	$kV = 10^{3} V$
100	$= 10^{2}$	hecto	h	$hm = 10^{2} m$
10	$= 10$	deka	da	$dam = 10 m$
0.1	$= 10^{-1}$	deci	d	$dm = 10^{-1} m$
0.01	$= 10^{-2}$	centi	c	$cm = 10^{-2} m$
0.001	$= 10^{-3}$	milli	m	$mA = 10^{-3} A$
0.000 001	$= 10^{-6}$	micro	μ	$\mu V = 10^{-6} V$
0.000 000 001	$= 10^{-9}$	nano	n	$ns - 10^{-9} s$
0.000 000 000 001	$= 10^{-12}$	pico	p	$pF = 10^{-12} F$

CONDUCTOR THICKNESS AND WIDTH

(For use in determining current carrying capacity and sizes of etched
copper conductors for various temperature rises above ambient)

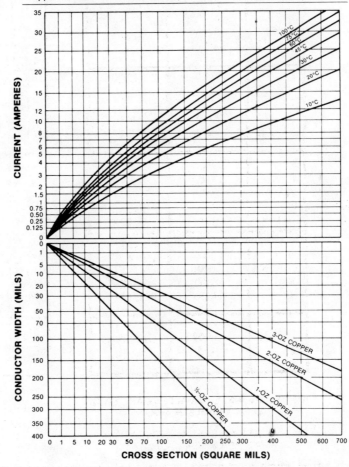

TEMPERATURE CONVERSION

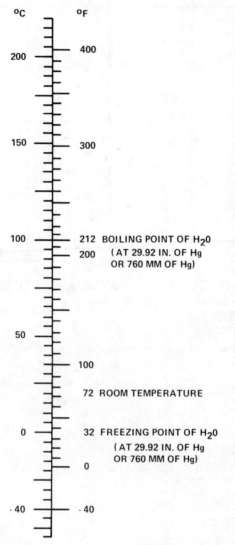

°C	°F	°C	°F
-70	-94	110	230
-60	-76	120	248
-50	-58	130	266
-40	-40	140	284
-30	-22	150	302
-20	- 4	160	320
-10	14	170	338
0	32	180	356
10	50	190	374
20	68	200	392
30	86	210	410
40	104	220	428
50	122	230	446
60	140	240	464
70	158	250	482
80	176	260	500
100	212	300	572

212 BOILING POINT OF H_2O
(AT 29.92 IN. OF Hg
OR 760 MM OF Hg)

72 ROOM TEMPERATURE

32 FREEZING POINT OF H_2O
(AT 29.92 IN. OF Hg
OR 760 MM OF Hg)

VISCOSITY INTERPRETATION

Listing viscosities by centipoise is sometimes confusing unless one is thoroughly familiar with this particular system. The following practical interpretation will be of assistance. The viscosity readings are for mixed compounds.

The readings were taken at 25°C with a Brookfield viscosimeter.

```
     1 CENTIPOISE (C.P.S.) - WATER
   400 CENTIPOISE (C.P.S.) - #10 MOTOR OIL
 1,000 CENTIPOISE (C.P.S.) - CASTOR OIL
 3,500 CENTIPOISE (C.P.S.) - KARO SYRUP
 4,500 CENTIPOISE (C.P.S.) - #40 MOTOR OIL
25,000 CENTIPOISE (C.P.S.) - HERSHEY CHOCOLATE SYRUP
```

To convert temperatures use following formulas:

$$°C = 5/9 \ (°F - 32)$$ (Celsius) Formerly Centigrade

$$°F = 9/5 \ (°C + 32)$$ (Fahrenheit)

$$°K = °C + 273.15$$ (Kelvin)

$$°R = °F + 459.67$$ (Rankin)

CONVERSION TABLES

1 hp = 746 watts = 33,000 ft-lb/min = 2,544 btu/hr 1 hp-hr = .746 kw-hr = 1,980,000 ft-lb = 2,545 btu = 273,740 kg meters 1 ft-lb = 1,356 joules = 1,3826 kg meters 1 watt = 1 joule/sec = 3.413 btu/hr = 44.22 ft-lb/min	1 in of water = .0361 lb per sq in = .0735 in of Hg 1 ft of water = .4332 lb per sq in = .8824 in of Hg 1 in of Hg = .4912 lb per sq in = 13.58 in of water = 1.131 ft of water 1 cm of Hg = .1934 lb per sq in 1 atm = 14,696 lb per sq in = 33.95 ft of water = 760 mm of Hg 1 lb per sq in = 27.71 in of water = 2.309 ft of water = 2.04 in of Hg = .06804 atm	1 kw = 1,000 watts = 1.34 hp = 44,240 ft-lb/min = 56.9 btu/min 1 kw hr = 1,000 watt hr = 1.34 hp-hr = 2,654,200 ft-lb = 3,413 btu = 3,600,000 joules 1 btu = 1052 watt sec = 778 ft-lb 1 joule = 1 watt sec = .73756 ft-lb
1 inch = 25.4 min 1 mm = .03937 in. 1 foot = 30.48 cm 1 meter = 39.37 in. = 3.28 ft 1 meter = 100 cm = 1000 mm 1 mile = 1.609 km 1 km = .6214 mile = 3/5 mile = 1000 meters		1 kg = 2.2 lb 1 cu in = 16.39 cu cm 1 cu ft = 1728 cu in 1 cu ft = 7.4805 US gal 1 US gal = .1337 cu ft 1 liter = 61.0 cu in = 1000 cu cm (cc) 1 liter = 1.0567 US qt
	1 sq in = 6.4516 sq cm 1 sq cm = .155 sq in 1 sq ft = 929.03 sq cm	
1 mile = 1,760 yd = 5,280 ft 1 sq mi = 640 acres 1 cir in = 1,000,000 cir mils	1 nautical mile = 6,080 ft 1 fathom = 6 ft	1 cu ft = 1.728 cu in 1 ounce = 437.5 grams = 28.35 grams

SURFACES AND VOLUME OF SOLIDS

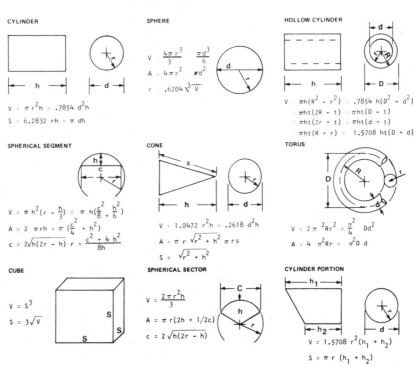

CYLINDER

$V = \pi r^2 h = .7854\ d^2 h$

$S = 6.2832\ rh = \pi\ dh$

SPHERE

$V = \dfrac{4 \pi r^3}{3} = \dfrac{\pi d^3}{6}$

$A = 4 \pi r^2 = \pi d^2$

$r = .6204 \sqrt[3]{V}$

HOLLOW CYLINDER

$V = \pi h(R^2 - r^2) = .7854\ h(D^2 - d^2)$

$= \pi ht(2R - t) = \pi ht(D - t)$

$= \pi ht(2r + t) = \pi ht(d + t)$

$= \pi ht(R + r) = 1.5708\ ht(D + d)$

SPHERICAL SEGMENT

$V = \pi h^2(r - \dfrac{h}{3}) = \pi\ h(\dfrac{c^2}{8} + \dfrac{h^2}{6})$

$A = 2\ \pi rh = \pi\ (\dfrac{c^2}{4} + h^2)$

$c = 2\sqrt{h(2r - h)}\quad r = \dfrac{c^2 + 4\ h^2}{8h}$

CONE

$V = 1.0472\ r^2 h = .2618\ d^2 h$

$A = \pi r \sqrt{r^2 + h^2}\ \pi rs$

$S = \sqrt{r^2 + h^2}$

TORUS

$V = 2 \pi^2 R r^2 = \dfrac{\pi^2}{4}\ D d^2$

$A = 4\ \pi^2 R r = \pi^2 D\ d$

CUBE

$V = S^3$

$S = 3\sqrt{V}$

SPHERICAL SECTOR

$V = \dfrac{2 \pi r^2 h}{3}$

$A = \pi r (2h + 1/2c)$

$c = 2 \sqrt{h(2r - h)}$

CYLINDER PORTION

$V = 1.5708\ r^2(h_1 + h_2)$

$S = \pi r\ (h_1 + h_2)$

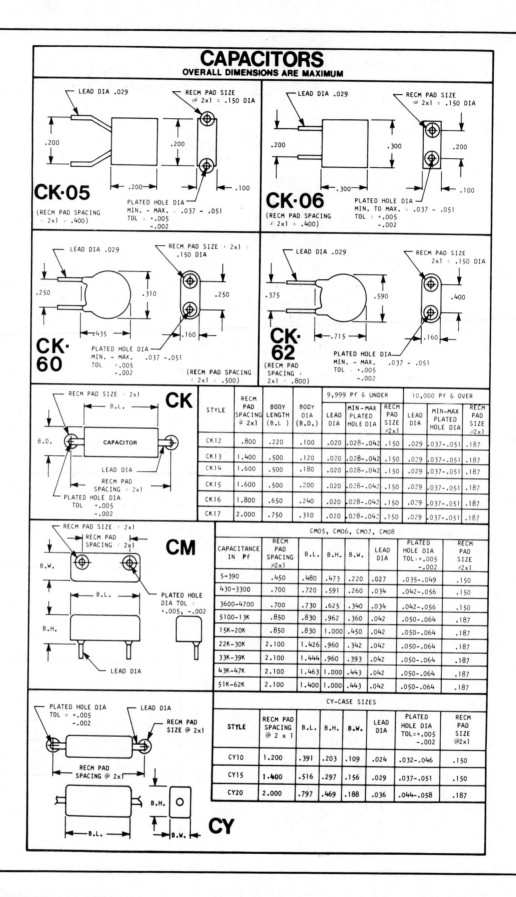

CAPACITORS
OVERALL DIMENSIONS ARE MAXIMUM

CK·05
(RECM PAD SPACING @ 2x1 = .400)

LEAD DIA .029
.200
.200
.200
RECM PAD SIZE @ 2x1 = .150 DIA
.200
.100
PLATED HOLE DIA
MIN. - MAX. .037 - .051
TOL = +.005
        -.002

CK·06
(RECM PAD SPACING @ 2x1 = .400)

LEAD DIA .029
.200
.300
.300
RECM PAD SIZE @ 2x1 = .150 DIA
.200
.100
PLATED HOLE DIA
MIN. TO MAX. = .037 - .051
TOL = +.005
        -.002

CK·60

LEAD DIA .029
.250
.310
.435
RECM PAD SIZE @ 2x1 = .150 DIA
.250
.160
PLATED HOLE DIA
MIN. - MAX. .037 -.051
TOL   +.005
        -.002
(RECM PAD SPACING @ 2x1 = .500)

CK·62
(RECM PAD SPACING @ 2x1 = .800)

LEAD DIA .029
.375
.590
.715
RECM PAD SIZE @ 2x1 = .150 DIA
.400
.160
PLATED HOLE DIA
MIN. - MAX. .037 - .051
TOL = +.005
        -.002

CK

RECM PAD SIZE @ 2x1
B.L.
B.D.
CAPACITOR
LEAD DIA
RECM PAD SPACING @ 2x1
PLATED HOLE DIA
TOL +.005
    -.002

| | | | | 9,999 Pf & UNDER | | | 10,000 Pf & OVER | | |
STYLE	RECM PAD SPACING @ 2x1	BODY LENGTH (B.L.)	BODY DIA (B.D.)	LEAD DIA	MIN-MAX PLATED HOLE DIA	RECM PAD SIZE @2x1	LEAD DIA	MIN-MAX PLATED HOLE DIA	RECM PAD SIZE @2x1
CK12	.800	.220	.100	.020	.028-.042	.150	.029	.037-.051	.187
CK13	1.400	.500	.120	.020	.028-.042	.150	.029	.037-.051	.187
CK14	1.600	.500	.180	.020	.028-.042	.150	.029	.037-.051	.187
CK15	1.600	.500	.200	.020	.028-.042	.150	.029	.037-.051	.187
CK16	1.800	.650	.240	.020	.028-.042	.150	.029	.037-.051	.187
CK17	2.000	.750	.310	.020	.028-.042	.150	.029	.037-.051	.187

CM

RECM PAD SIZE @ 2x1
RECM PAD SPACING @ 2x1
B.W.
B.L.
B.H.
PLATED HOLE DIA TOL +.005, -.002
LEAD DIA

| | CM05, CM06, CM07, CM08 | | | | | | |
CAPACITANCE IN Pf	RECM PAD SPACING @2x1	B.L.	B.H.	B.W.	LEAD DIA	PLATED HOLE DIA TOL=+.005 -.002	RECM PAD SIZE @2x1
5-390	.450	.480	.473	.220	.027	.035-.049	.150
430-3300	.700	.720	.591	.260	.034	.042-.056	.150
3600-4700	.700	.730	.625	.340	.034	.042-.056	.150
5100-13K	.850	.830	.962	.360	.042	.050-.064	.187
15K-20K	.850	.830	1.000	.450	.042	.050-.064	.187
22K-30K	2.100	1.426	.960	.342	.042	.050-.064	.187
33K-39K	2.100	1.444	.960	.393	.042	.050-.064	.187
43K-47K	2.100	1.463	1.000	.443	.042	.050-.064	.187
51K-62K	2.100	1.400	1.000	.443	.042	.050-.064	.187

CY

PLATED HOLE DIA TOL = +.005, -.002
LEAD DIA
RECM PAD SIZE @ 2x1
RECM PAD SPACING @ 2x1
B.H.
B.L.
B.W.

| | CY-CASE SIZES | | | | | | |
STYLE	RECM PAD SPACING @ 2 x 1	B.L.	B.H.	B.W.	LEAD DIA	PLATED HOLE DIA TOL=+.005 -.002	RECM PAD SIZE @2x1
CY10	1.200	.391	.203	.109	.024	.032-.046	.150
CY15	1.400	.516	.297	.156	.029	.037-.051	.150
CY20	2.000	.797	.469	.188	.036	.044-.058	.187

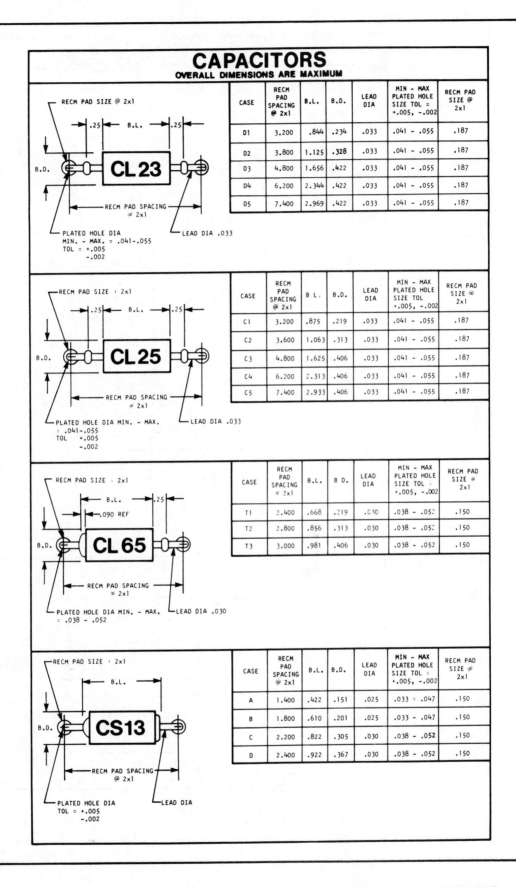

CAPACITORS
OVERALL DIMENSIONS ARE MAXIMUM

CL 23

CASE	RECM PAD SPACING @ 2x1	B.L.	B.D.	LEAD DIA	MIN - MAX PLATED HOLE SIZE TOL = +.005, -.002	RECM PAD SIZE @ 2x1
D1	3.200	.844	.234	.033	.041 - .055	.187
D2	3.800	1.125	.328	.033	.041 - .055	.187
D3	4.800	1.656	.422	.033	.041 - .055	.187
D4	6.200	2.344	.422	.033	.041 - .055	.187
D5	7.400	2.969	.422	.033	.041 - .055	.187

CL 25

CASE	RECM PAD SPACING @ 2x1	B.L.	B.D.	LEAD DIA	MIN - MAX PLATED HOLE SIZE TOL +.005, -.002	RECM PAD SIZE @ 2x1
C1	3.200	.875	.219	.033	.041 - .055	.187
C2	3.600	1.063	.313	.033	.041 - .055	.187
C3	4.800	1.625	.406	.033	.041 - .055	.187
C4	6.200	2.313	.406	.033	.041 - .055	.187
C5	7.400	2.933	.406	.033	.041 - .055	.187

CL 65

CASE	RECM PAD SPACING @ 2x1	B.L.	B.D.	LEAD DIA	MIN - MAX PLATED HOLE SIZE TOL = +.005, -.002	RECM PAD SIZE @ 2x1
T1	2.400	.668	.219	.030	.038 - .052	.150
T2	2.800	.856	.313	.030	.038 - .052	.150
T3	3.000	.981	.406	.030	.038 - .052	.150

CS 13

CASE	RECM PAD SPACING @ 2x1	B.L.	B.D.	LEAD DIA	MIN - MAX PLATED HOLE SIZE TOL = +.005, -.002	RECM PAD SIZE @ 2x1
A	1.400	.422	.151	.025	.033 - .047	.150
B	1.800	.610	.201	.025	.033 - .047	.150
C	2.200	.822	.305	.030	.038 - .052	.150
D	2.400	.922	.367	.030	.038 - .052	.150

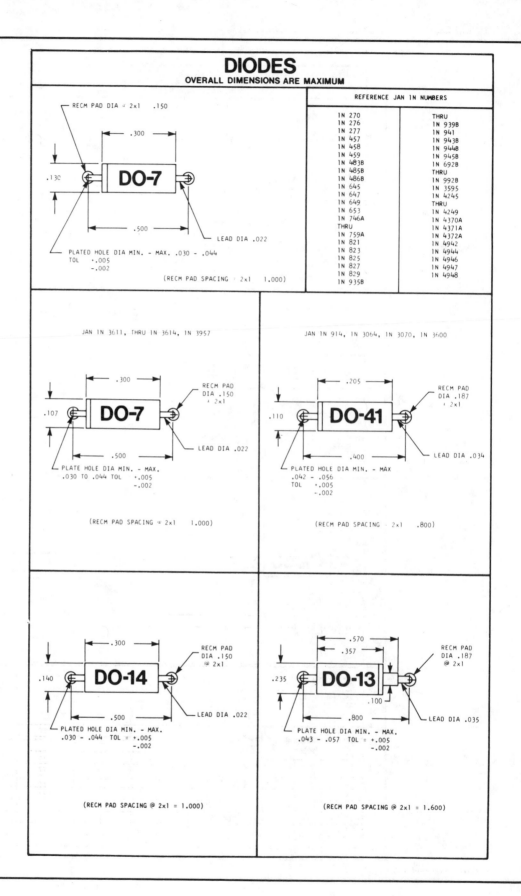

DIODES
OVERALL DIMENSIONS ARE MAXIMUM

RECM PAD DIA @ 2x1 .150

.300

DO-7

.130

.500

LEAD DIA .022

PLATED HOLE DIA MIN. - MAX. .030 - .044
TOL +.005
     -.002

(RECM PAD SPACING @ 2x1   1.000)

REFERENCE JAN 1N NUMBERS	
1N 270	THRU
1N 276	1N 939B
1N 277	1N 941
1N 457	1N 943B
1N 458	1N 944B
1N 459	1N 945B
1N 483B	1N 692B
1N 485B	THRU
1N 486B	1N 992B
1N 645	1N 3595
1N 647	1N 4245
1N 649	THRU
1N 653	1N 4249
1N 746A	1N 4370A
THRU	1N 4371A
1N 759A	1N 4372A
1N 821	1N 4942
1N 823	1N 4944
1N 825	1N 4946
1N 827	1N 4947
1N 829	1N 4948
1N 935B	

JAN 1N 3611, THRU 1N 3614, 1N 3957

.300

DO-7

.107

RECM PAD
DIA .150
@ 2x1

.500

LEAD DIA .022

PLATE HOLE DIA MIN. - MAX.
.030 TO .044 TOL +.005
                   -.002

(RECM PAD SPACING @ 2x1   1.000)

JAN 1N 914, 1N 3064, 1N 3070, 1N 3600

.205

DO-41

.110

RECM PAD
DIA .187
@ 2x1

.400

LEAD DIA .034

PLATED HOLE DIA MIN. - MAX.
.042 - .056
TOL +.005
     -.002

(RECM PAD SPACING @ 2x1   .800)

.300

DO-14

.140

RECM PAD
DIA .150
@ 2x1

.500

LEAD DIA .022

PLATED HOLE DIA MIN. - MAX.
.030 - .044 TOL = +.005
                  -.002

(RECM PAD SPACING @ 2x1 = 1.000)

.570

.357

DO-13

.235

RECM PAD
DIA .187
@ 2x1

.100

.800

LEAD DIA .035

PLATE HOLE DIA MIN. - MAX.
.043 - .057 TOL = +.005
                   -.002

(RECM PAD SPACING @ 2x1 = 1.600)

RESISTORS

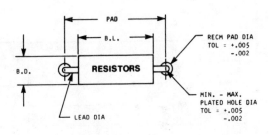

OVERALL DIMENSIONS ARE MAXIMUM

STYLE	WATT	PAD 2 x 1	RECM PAD DIA 2 x 1	BODY LENGTH (B.L.)	BODY DIA (B.D.)	LEAD DIA	MIN. - MAX. PLATED HOLE DIA TOL = +.005 / -.002
RC05	1/8	.800	.150	.160	.066	.018	.026 - .040
RC06	1/10	.800	.150	.160	.075	.018	.026 - .040
RC07	1/4	1.000	.150	.281	.098	.027	.035 - .049
RC08	1/10	.800	.150	.225	.115	.018	.026 - .040
RC12	1/4	1.200	.150	.390	.148	.028	.036 - .050
RC20	1/2	1.200	.187	.416	.161	.036	.044 - .058
RC22	1/2	1.600	.187	.575	.233	.036	.044 - .058
RC32	1	1.600	.187	.593	.240	.042	.050 - .064
RC42	2	2.000	.200	.728	.336	.048	.056 - .070
RL05	1/8	.800	.150	.170	.070	.017	.025 - .040
RL07	1/4	1.000	.150	.281	.098	.027	.035 - .049
RL20	1/2	1.200	.187	.416	.161	.036	.044 - .058
RL32	1	1.600	.187	.593	.205	.042	.050 - .064
RL42	2	2.000	.200	.728	.336	.050	.058 - .072
RN50	1/10	.800	.150	.170	.080	.018	.026 - .040
RN55	1/10	1.000	.150	.281	.141	.027	.035 - .049
RN60	1/8	1.200	.150	.437	.165	.027	.035 - .049
RN65	1/4	1.800	.150	.656	.250	.027	.035 - .049
RN70	1/2	2.200	.187	.875	.328	.034	.042 - .056
RN75	1	2.800	.187	1.125	.437	.034	.042 - .056
RN80	2	5.000	.187	2.281	.437	.034	.042 - .056
RWP20	3	1.600	.187	.563	.250	.036	.044 - .058

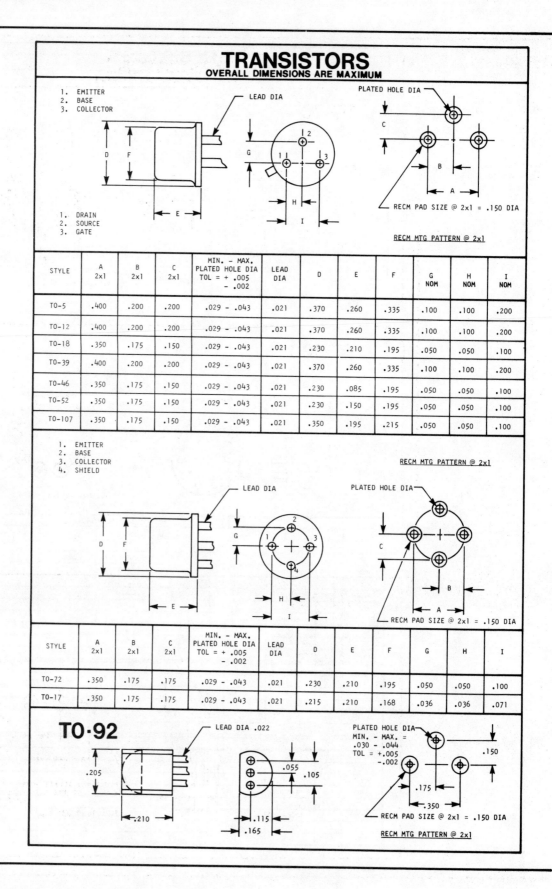

TRANSISTORS
OVERALL DIMENSIONS ARE MAXIMUM

1. EMITTER
2. BASE
3. COLLECTOR

1. DRAIN
2. SOURCE
3. GATE

LEAD DIA

PLATED HOLE DIA

RECM PAD SIZE @ 2x1 = .150 DIA

RECM MTG PATTERN @ 2x1

STYLE	A 2x1	B 2x1	C 2x1	MIN. - MAX. PLATED HOLE DIA TOL = + .005 - .002	LEAD DIA	D	E	F	G NOM	H NOM	I NOM
TO-5	.400	.200	.200	.029 - .043	.021	.370	.260	.335	.100	.100	.200
TO-12	.400	.200	.200	.029 - .043	.021	.370	.260	.335	.100	.100	.200
TO-18	.350	.175	.150	.029 - .043	.021	.230	.210	.195	.050	.050	.100
TO-39	.400	.200	.200	.029 - .043	.021	.370	.260	.335	.100	.100	.200
TO-46	.350	.175	.150	.029 - .043	.021	.230	.085	.195	.050	.050	.100
TO-52	.350	.175	.150	.029 - .043	.021	.230	.150	.195	.050	.050	.100
TO-107	.350	.175	.150	.029 - .043	.021	.350	.195	.215	.050	.050	.100

1. EMITTER
2. BASE
3. COLLECTOR
4. SHIELD

RECM MTG PATTERN @ 2x1

LEAD DIA

PLATED HOLE DIA

RECM PAD SIZE @ 2x1 = .150 DIA

STYLE	A 2x1	B 2x1	C 2x1	MIN. - MAX. PLATED HOLE DIA TOL = + .005 - .002	LEAD DIA	D	E	F	G	H	I
TO-72	.350	.175	.175	.029 - .043	.021	.230	.210	.195	.050	.050	.100
TO-17	.350	.175	.175	.029 - .043	.021	.215	.210	.168	.036	.036	.071

TO-92

LEAD DIA .022

PLATED HOLE DIA MIN. - MAX. = .030 - .044 TOL = +.005 -.002

.205

.210

.055
.105
.115
.165

.150
.175
.350

RECM PAD SIZE @ 2x1 = .150 DIA

RECM MTG PATTERN @ 2x1

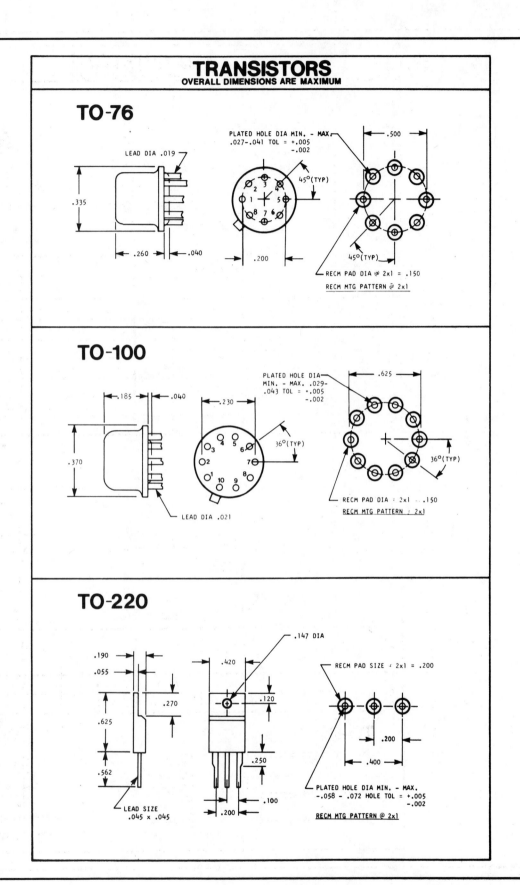

TRANSISTORS
OVERALL DIMENSIONS ARE MAXIMUM

TO-76

LEAD DIA .019

.335

.260   .040

PLATED HOLE DIA MIN. - MAX
.027-.041 TOL = +.005
                    -.002

45°(TYP)

.500

.200

45°(TYP)

RECM PAD DIA @ 2x1 = .150
RECM MTG PATTERN @ 2x1

TO-100

.185   .040

.230

.370

LEAD DIA .021

PLATED HOLE DIA
MIN. - MAX. .029-
.043 TOL = +.005
            -.002

.625

36°(TYP)

36°(TYP)

RECM PAD DIA : 2x1 - .150
RECM MTG PATTERN : 2x1

TO-220

.190
.055

.270

.625

.562

LEAD SIZE
.045 x .045

.147 DIA

.420

.120

.250

.100

.200

RECM PAD SIZE @ 2x1 = .200

.200

.400

PLATED HOLE DIA MIN. - MAX.
-.058 - .072 HOLE TOL = +.005
                        -.002

RECM MTG PATTERN @ 2x1

FUNDAMENTAL RULES FOR DIMENSIONING

1. Show enough dimensions so that the intended sizes and shapes can be determined without calculating or assuming any distances.

2. State each dimension clearly so that it can be interpreted in only one way.

3. SHOW THE DIMENSIONS BETWEEN POINTS, LINES, OR SURFACES WHICH HAVE A NECESSARY AND SPECIFIC RELATION TO EACH OTHER OR WHICH CONTROL THE LOCATION OF OTHER COMPONENTS OR MATING PARTS.

4. Select and arrange dimensions to avoid accumulations of tolerances that may permit various interpretations and cause unsatisfactory mating of parts and failure in use.

5. Show each dimension only once.

6. Where possible, dimension each feature in the view where it appears in profile and where its true shape is evident.

7. Do not show dimensions to lines representing hidden surfaces.

APPROXIMATE SURFACE ROUGHNESS

USE OF SURFACE ROUGHNESS SYMBOLS

The roughness of any surface, except cast surfaces, may be expressed by the use of symbols and numerical ratings. The finish mark symbols are used to designate the applicable surface. The numerical rating indicates the roughness of that surface.

CONTROL OF SURFACE ROUGHNESS

The roughness of any surface is determined by design requirements rather than by production processes; however, overcontrol will increase the cost of production. Therefore, specify surface roughness control on drawings only when it is essential to the appearance or mechanical performance of the product.

TYPICAL SURFACE ROUGHNESS CHART

Castings: Do not use symbols and ratings on cast surfaces.
Mill Cleanup and Shear Cuts..250 to 125
Machining:
    .001 to .005 Tolerance. 63
    .0005 to .001 Tolerance 32
    .0002 to .0005 Tolerance. 16
    .0000 to .0002 Tolerance. 8

FINISH MARK SYMBOL AND ROUGHNESS HEIGHT RATING.

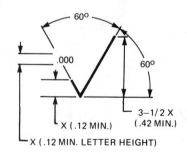

CLEARANCE HOLES FOR THREADED FASTENERS

THREAD SIZE	TOLERANCE BETWEEN HOLE CENTERS		
	±.005	±.010	±.020
0	.076 DIA (#48)		
1	.089 DIA (#43)	.102 DIA (#38)	.128 DIA (#30)*
2	.102 DIA (#38)	.116 DIA (#32)	.144 DIA (#27)*
4	.125 DIA (#1/8)	.140 DIA (#28)	.166 DIA (#19)*
6	.150 DIA (#25)	.166 DIA (#19)	.191 DIA (#11)*
8	.177 DIA (#16)	.189 DIA (#12)	.219 DIA (#7/32)*
10	.199 DIA (#8)	.213 DIA (#3)	.242 DIA (C)
1/4	.257 DIA (F)	.272 DIA (I)	.302 DIA (N)

*Exclude Fillister and socket head cap screws.
FLAT WASHERS WILL BE REQUIRED WITH ±.020 TOLERANCE.

NOTES:

1. This chart applies to the following:

    a. Where a row of holes is on the same centerline.

    b. Where the holes are on more than one centerline.

    c. Where clearance holes are in both parts.

    d. Where clearance holes are in one part and tapped holes or studs are in the other part.

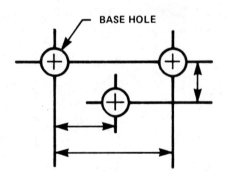

All dimensioning shall be from an established base hole or fixed point.

2. This chart does not apply to the following:

    a. Clearance holes for rivets.

    b. One fastener used independent of any other.

    c. Clearance holes for flat head machine screws.

3. The hole sizes listed have been formulated for the most severe conditions for screw fasteners and represent a noninterference probability of approximately 98%.

PREFERRED BEND RADII FOR STRAIGHT BENDS IN SHEET METALS

SHEET THICKNESS	ALUMINUM						
	2024 T3	5052 0	5052 H32	5052 H34	6061 0	6061 T4	6061 T6 (See Note 1)
.020	.06	.03	.03	.03*	.03	.06	.06
.025	.06	.03	.03	.03*	.03*	.06	.06
.032	.09*	.03	.06	.06*	.03*	.09	.09*
.040	.12	.06*	.06	.06*	.06	.12	.12*
.050	.16	.06	.09	.09*	.06*	.16	.16*
.063	.19*	.06	.09*	.09*	.06*	.19	.19*
.080	.25	.09	.12*	.12	.09	.25	.25*
.090	.31*	.09	.12*	.12	.09	.31	.31*
.100	.38	.12	.19	.19	.12	.38	.38
.125	.50*	.12	.19*	.19	.12	.50	.50*
.160	.75	.16	.25	.25	.16	.62	.62
.190	1.00*	.19	.37*	.37	.19	.84	.87*

SHEET THICKNESS	STEEL		
	CORROSION RESISTANT		PLAIN CARBON
	TYPES 301 302 304 (Annealed)	TYPES 301 302 304 (1/4 H)	
.020			.06
.025			.06
.032			.06
.040			.09
.050			.09
.063			.09
.080			.12
.090			.12
.100			.16
.125			.19
.160			.25
.190			.31
.020-.040	.03	.06	
.045-.070	.06	.12	
.075-.105	.09	.19	
.110-.135	.12	.25	

NOTES:

1. If 6061-T6 material is used and the minimum bend radii shown is too large, the option is to anneal the material, form the bend, and then heat treat the material to the T6 condition again.

2. *Represents "common stock" material.

3. Shops require .010 tolerance for each bend.

DISSIMILAR METALS

Without proper protective coating, do not use a metal from one group in contact with a metal listed in another group:

1. Tin, cadmium and zinc may be used with all metals in Groups II and III.

2. Stainless steel may be used with all metals in Groups II, III and IV.

Use metals within each group together.
MIL-STD-454

GROUP I	GROUP II	GROUP III	GROUP IV
MAGNESIUM ALLOYS	ALUMINUM	ZINC	COPPER AND ITS ALLOYS
TIN	ALUMINUM ALLOYS	CADMIUM	NICKEL AND ITS ALLOYS
Al ALLOY (5052)	ZINC	STEEL	CHROMIUM
Al ALLOY (5056)	CADMIUM	LEAD	STAINLESS STEEL
Al ALLOY (5356)	TIN	TIN	GOLD
		TIN LEAD (SOLDER)	
Al ALLOY (6061)	STAINLESS STEEL	STAINLESS STEEL	SILVER
Al ALLOY (6063)	TIN LEAD (SOLDER)	NICKEL AND ITS ALLOYS	

KNURL DATA

For decoration or gripping application, specify pitch and type. Add "Before" and "After Knurling" dimensions to call-out when application is for a press fit between two parts.

REF: USAS Y14.5-1966, USAS B94.6-1966

TYPE	DIAMETRAL PITCH	INCREASE IN PART DIAMETER WHEN KNURLED (APPROX.)
DIAMOND	160 DP (Fine) 128 DP (Med) 96 DP (Coarse)*	.009 .012 .016
DIAGONAL (PLAIN SPIRAL)	160 DP (Fine) 128 DP (Med) 96 DP (Coarse)*	.009 .012 .016
STRAIGHT (90° Vee)	160 DP (Fine) 128 DP (Med) 96 DP (Coarse)*	.009 .012 .016

* Preferred Diametral Pitch

RIVETS

RIVET DIA	PILOT DRILL	BODY DRILL	100° CSK RIVET		UNIVERSAL HD
			±.004 HEAD DIA	CSK DIA	HEAD DIA
1/16	–	.067 (#51)	.114	.114	.125
3/32	–	.098 (#40)	.179	.179	.187
1/8	.098 (#40)	.128 (#30)	.225	.225	.250
5/32	.098 (#40)	.159 (#21)	.286	.286	.312
3/16	.098 (#40)	.191 (#11)	.353	.353	.375
1/4	.098 (#40)	.257 (F)	.476	.476	.500

NOTES:

1. Mating parts to be riveted in assembly should have all predrilled pilot holes in one of the mating parts. Selection of part to be predrilled may be determined by:

   a. Accessibility for hand drilling.

   b. The part that has the greater material thickness.

   c. The material of greater hardness.

2. Pilot holes for rivets 1/8 diameter or more shall be .098 Dia (#40).

3. Rivet Diameter:

   Maximum – 3 times thickness of material to be riveted.

   Minimum – Thickness of material to be riveted.

4. Minimum Edge Distance from Center of Rivet:

   2 times diameter of rivet.

5. SELECTING RIVET LENGTH

   SUM OF MATERIAL THICKNESS PLUS 1-1/2 TIMES DIAMETER OF RIVET (FOR UPSETTING HEAD); TO NEAREST 1/16-INCH INCREMENT SHORTER THAN MAXIMUM CALCULATED LENGTH.

6. Types of Commonly Used Rivets

   UNIVERSAL HD (Aluminum) – TI 411175; MS 20470 (Preferred usage)

   100° CSK HD (Aluminum) – TI 411172; MS 20426

   UNIVERSAL HD (Steel, Carbon, and Steel Corrosion-Resistant) – TI 416918; MS 20613

   UNIVERSAL HD (Brass, Copper and Nickel-Copper Alloy) – TI 418180; MS 20615

   Tubular, Oval HD (Aluminum, Steel, Brass, Monel) – TI 411059; MS 16535

0·80

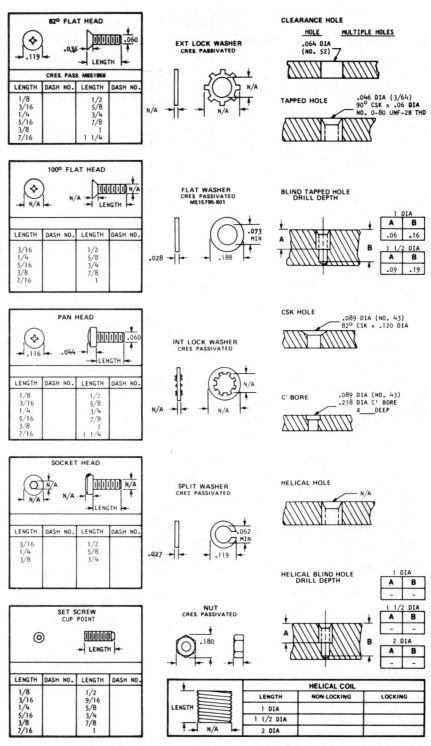

82° FLAT HEAD

CRES. PASS. MS51959

LENGTH	DASH NO.	LENGTH	DASH NO.
1/8		1/2	
3/16		5/8	
1/4		3/4	
5/16		7/8	
3/8		1	
7/16		1 1/4	

.119   .036   .060   LENGTH

100° FLAT HEAD

N/A   N/A   LENGTH

LENGTH	DASH NO.	LENGTH	DASH NO.
3/16		1/2	
1/4		5/8	
5/16		3/4	
3/8		7/8	
7/16		1	

PAN HEAD

.116   .044   .060   LENGTH

LENGTH	DASH NO.	LENGTH	DASH NO.
1/8		1/2	
3/16		5/8	
1/4		3/4	
5/16		7/8	
3/8		1	
7/16		1 1/4	

SOCKET HEAD

N/A   N/A   N/A   LENGTH

LENGTH	DASH NO.	LENGTH	DASH NO.
3/16		1/2	
1/4		5/8	
3/8		3/4	

SET SCREW
CUP POINT

LENGTH

LENGTH	DASH NO.	LENGTH	DASH NO.
1/8		1/2	
3/16		9/16	
1/4		5/8	
5/16		3/4	
3/8		7/8	
7/16		1	

EXT LOCK WASHER
CRES. PASSIVATED

N/A   N/A

FLAT WASHER
CRES PASSIVATED
MS15795-801

.028   .073 MIN   .188

INT LOCK WASHER
CRES. PASSIVATED

N/A   N/A

SPLIT WASHER
CRES. PASSIVATED

.027   .062 MIN   .119

NUT
CRES. PASSIVATED

.180

CLEARANCE HOLE

HOLE	MULTIPLE HOLES

.064 DIA (NO. 52)

TAPPED HOLE

.046 DIA (3/64)
90° CSK x .06 DIA
NO. 0-80 UNF-2B THD

BLIND TAPPED HOLE
DRILL DEPTH

A   B

1 DIA	
A	B
.06	.16

1 1/2 DIA	
A	B
.09	.19

CSK HOLE

.089 DIA (NO. 43)
82° CSK x .120 DIA

C' BORE

.089 DIA (NO. 43)
.218 DIA C' BORE
X____ DEEP

HELICAL HOLE

N/A

HELICAL BLIND HOLE
DRILL DEPTH

A   B

1 DIA	
A	B
-	-

1 1/2 DIA	
A	B
-	-

2 DIA	
A	B
-	-

HELICAL COIL		
LENGTH	NON-LOCKING	LOCKING
1 DIA		
1 1/2 DIA		
2 DIA		

LENGTH   N/A

ALL DIMENSIONS MAXIMUM UNLESS OTHERWISE SPECIFIED

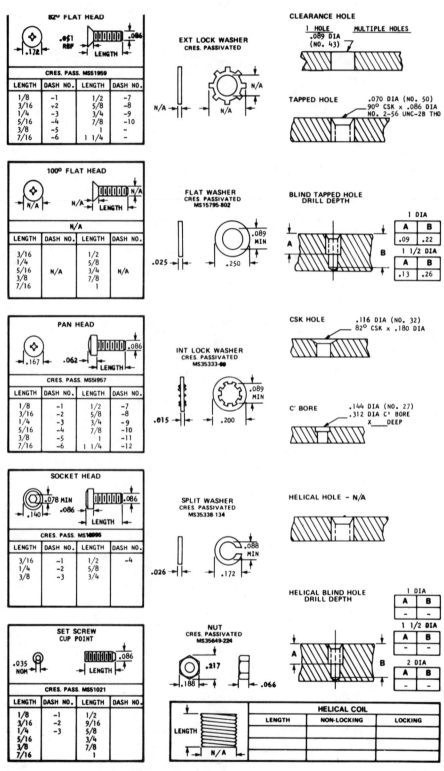

82° FLAT HEAD

.051 REF · .172 · .086 · LENGTH

CRES. PASS. MS51959			
LENGTH	DASH NO.	LENGTH	DASH NO.
1/8	-1	1/2	-7
3/16	-2	5/8	-8
1/4	-3	3/4	-9
5/16	-4	7/8	-10
3/8	-5	1	-
7/16	-6	1 1/4	-

100° FLAT HEAD

N/A · LENGTH · N/A

N/A			
LENGTH	DASH NO.	LENGTH	DASH NO.
3/16		1/2	
1/4		5/8	
5/16	N/A	3/4	N/A
3/8		7/8	
7/16		1	

PAN HEAD

.167 · .062 · LENGTH · .086

CRES. PASS. MS51957			
LENGTH	DASH NO.	LENGTH	DASH NO.
1/8	-1	1/2	-7
3/16	-2	5/8	-8
1/4	-3	3/4	-9
5/16	-4	7/8	-10
3/8	-5	1	-11
7/16	-6	1 1/4	-12

SOCKET HEAD

.078 MIN · .086 · .140 · LENGTH · .086

CRES. PASS. MS16995			
LENGTH	DASH NO.	LENGTH	DASH NO.
3/16	-1	1/2	-4
1/4	-2	5/8	
3/8	-3	3/4	

SET SCREW CUP POINT

.035 NOM · LENGTH · .086

CRES. PASS. MS51021			
LENGTH	DASH NO.	LENGTH	DASH NO.
1/8	-1	1/2	
3/16	-2	9/16	
1/4	-3	5/8	
5/16		3/4	
3/8		7/8	
7/16		1	

EXT LOCK WASHER
CRES. PASSIVATED

N/A · N/A

FLAT WASHER
CRES. PASSIVATED
MS15795-802

.025 · .089 MIN · .250

INT LOCK WASHER
CRES. PASSIVATED
MS35333-00

.015 · .089 MIN · .200

SPLIT WASHER
CRES. PASSIVATED
MS35338-134

.026 · .088 MIN · .172

NUT
CRES. PASSIVATED
MS35649-224

.217 · .188 · .066

CLEARANCE HOLE

1 HOLE .089 DIA (NO. 43) · MULTIPLE HOLES

TAPPED HOLE

.070 DIA (NO. 50)
90° CSK x .086 DIA
NO. 2-56 UNC-2B THD

BLIND TAPPED HOLE DRILL DEPTH

1 DIA	
A	B
.09	.22

1 1/2 DIA	
A	B
.13	.26

CSK HOLE

.116 DIA (NO. 32)
82° CSK x .180 DIA

C' BORE

.144 DIA (NO. 27)
.312 DIA C' BORE
X___DEEP

HELICAL HOLE - N/A

HELICAL BLIND HOLE DRILL DEPTH

1 DIA	
A	B
-	-

1 1/2 DIA	
A	B
-	-

2 DIA	
A	B
-	-

LENGTH · N/A

HELICAL COIL		
LENGTH	NON-LOCKING	LOCKING

ALL DIMENSIONS ARE MAXIMUM UNLESS OTHERWISE SPECIFIED

4·40

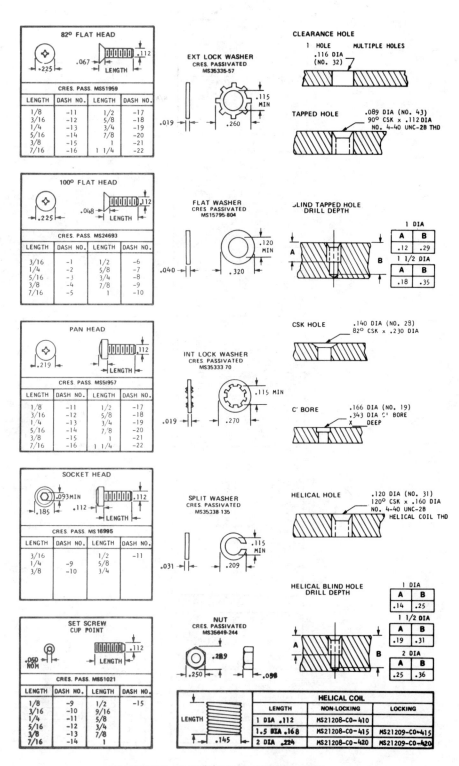

82° FLAT HEAD

.225   .067   .112   LENGTH

CRES. PASS. MS51959

LENGTH	DASH NO.	LENGTH	DASH NO.
1/8	-11	1/2	-17
3/16	-12	5/8	-18
1/4	-13	3/4	-19
5/16	-14	7/8	-20
3/8	-15	1	-21
7/16	-16	1 1/4	-22

100° FLAT HEAD

.225   .048   .112   LENGTH

CRES. PASS. MS24693

LENGTH	DASH NO.	LENGTH	DASH NO.
3/16	-1	1/2	-6
1/4	-2	5/8	-7
5/16	-3	3/4	-8
3/8	-4	7/8	-9
7/16	-5	1	-10

PAN HEAD

.219   .112   LENGTH

CRES. PASS. MS51957

LENGTH	DASH NO.	LENGTH	DASH NO.
1/8	-11	1/2	-17
3/16	-12	5/8	-18
1/4	-13	3/4	-19
5/16	-14	7/8	-20
3/8	-15	1	-21
7/16	-16	1 1/4	-22

SOCKET HEAD

.093MIN   .185   .112   .112   LENGTH

CRES. PASS. MS16995

LENGTH	DASH NO.	LENGTH	DASH NO.
3/16		1/2	-11
1/4	-9	5/8	
3/8	-10	3/4	

SET SCREW CUP POINT

.050 NOM   .112   LENGTH

CRES. PASS. MS51021

LENGTH	DASH NO.	LENGTH	DASH NO.
1/8	-9	1/2	-15
3/16	-10	9/16	
1/4	-11	5/8	
5/16	-12	3/4	
3/8	-13	7/8	
7/16	-14	1	

EXT LOCK WASHER
CRES. PASSIVATED MS35335-57

.019   .115 MIN   .260

FLAT WASHER
CRES PASSIVATED MS15795-804

.040   .120 MIN   .320

INT LOCK WASHER
CRES. PASSIVATED MS35333-70

.019   .115 MIN   .270

SPLIT WASHER
CRES PASSIVATED MS35338-135

.031   .115 MIN   .209

NUT
CRES. PASSIVATED MS35649-244

.289   .250   .098

CLEARANCE HOLE

1 HOLE   MULTIPLE HOLES
.116 DIA (NO. 32)

TAPPED HOLE

.089 DIA (NO. 43)
90° CSK x .112 DIA
NO. 4-40 UNC-2B THD

BLIND TAPPED HOLE
DRILL DEPTH

	1 DIA	
	A	B
	.12	.29

	1 1/2 DIA	
	A	B
	.18	.35

CSK HOLE

.140 DIA (NO. 28)
82° CSK x .230 DIA

C' BORE

.166 DIA (NO. 19)
.343 DIA C' BORE
X DEEP

HELICAL HOLE

.120 DIA (NO. 31)
120° CSK x .160 DIA
NO. 4-40 UNC-2B
HELICAL COIL THD

HELICAL BLIND HOLE
DRILL DEPTH

	1 DIA	
	A	B
	.14	.25

	1 1/2 DIA	
	A	B
	.19	.31

	2 DIA	
	A	B
	.25	.36

	HELICAL COIL		
LENGTH	LENGTH	NON-LOCKING	LOCKING
	1 DIA .112	MS21208-C0-410	
	1.5 DIA .168	MS21208-C0-415	MS21209-C0-415
	2 DIA .224	MS21208-C0-420	MS21209-C0-420

.145

ALL DIMENSIONS ARE MAXIMUM UNLESS OTHERWISE SPECIFIED

6·32

ALL DIMENSIONS ARE MAXIMUM UNLESS OTHERWISE SPECIFIED

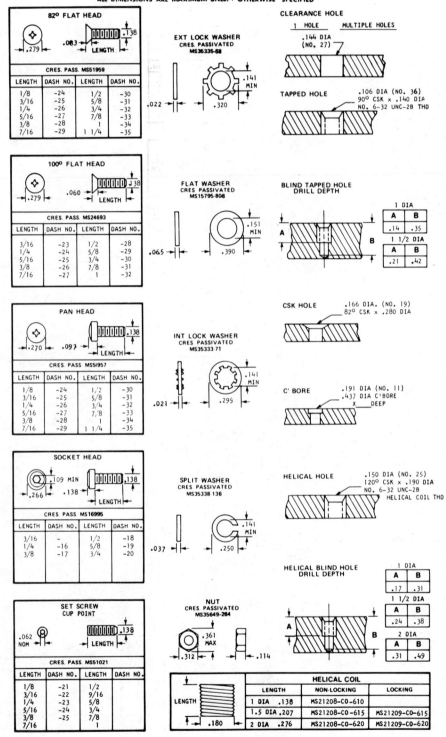

82° FLAT HEAD

.279 | .083 | .138 LENGTH

CRES. PASS. MS51959

LENGTH	DASH NO.	LENGTH	DASH NO.
1/8	-24	1/2	-30
3/16	-25	5/8	-31
1/4	-26	3/4	-32
5/16	-27	7/8	-33
3/8	-28	1	-34
7/16	-29	1 1/4	-35

100° FLAT HEAD

.279 | .060 | .138 LENGTH

CRES. PASS. MS24693

LENGTH	DASH NO.	LENGTH	DASH NO.
3/16	-23	1/2	-28
1/4	-24	5/8	-29
5/16	-25	3/4	-30
3/8	-26	7/8	-31
7/16	-27	1	-32

PAN HEAD

.270 | .097 | .138 LENGTH

CRES. PASS. MS51957

LENGTH	DASH NO.	LENGTH	DASH NO.
1/8	-24	1/2	-30
3/16	-25	5/8	-31
1/4	-26	3/4	-32
5/16	-27	7/8	-33
3/8	-28	1	-34
7/16	-29	1 1/4	-35

SOCKET HEAD

.109 MIN | .266 | .138 | .138 LENGTH

CRES. PASS. MS16995

LENGTH	DASH NO.	LENGTH	DASH NO.
3/16	-	1/2	-18
1/4	-16	5/8	-19
3/8	-17	3/4	-20

SET SCREW CUP POINT

.062 NOM | .138 LENGTH

CRES. PASS. MS51021

LENGTH	DASH NO.	LENGTH	DASH NO.
1/8	-21	1/2	
3/16	-22	9/16	
1/4	-23	5/8	
5/16	-24	3/4	
3/8	-25	7/8	
7/16		1	

EXT LOCK WASHER
CRES. PASSIVATED
MS35335-58

.022 | .320 | .141 MIN

FLAT WASHER
CRES. PASSIVATED
MS15795-806

.065 | .390 | .151 MIN

INT LOCK WASHER
CRES PASSIVATED
MS35333-71

.021 | .295 | .141 MIN

SPLIT WASHER
CRES PASSIVATED
MS35338 136

.037 | .250 | .141 MIN

NUT
CRES. PASSIVATED
MS35649-264

.361 MAX | .312 | .114

CLEARANCE HOLE

1 HOLE — MULTIPLE HOLES

.144 DIA (NO. 27)

TAPPED HOLE

.106 DIA (NO. 36)
90° CSK x .140 DIA
NO. 6-32 UNC-2B THD

BLIND TAPPED HOLE DRILL DEPTH

A / B

1 DIA	
A	B
.14	.35

1 1/2 DIA	
A	B
.21	.42

CSK HOLE

.166 DIA. (NO. 19)
82° CSK x .280 DIA

C' BORE

.191 DIA (NO. 11)
.437 DIA C'BORE
X DEEP

HELICAL HOLE

.150 DIA (NO. 25)
120° CSK x .190 DIA
NO. 6-32 UNC-2B
HELICAL COIL THD

HELICAL BLIND HOLE DRILL DEPTH

A / B

1 DIA	
A	B
.17	.31

1 1/2 DIA	
A	B
.24	.38

2 DIA	
A	B
.31	.49

LENGTH | .180

HELICAL COIL		
LENGTH	NON-LOCKING	LOCKING
1 DIA .138	MS21208-CO-610	
1.5 DIA .207	MS21208-CO-615	MS21209-CO-615
2 DIA .276	MS21208-CO-620	MS21209-CO-620

8·32

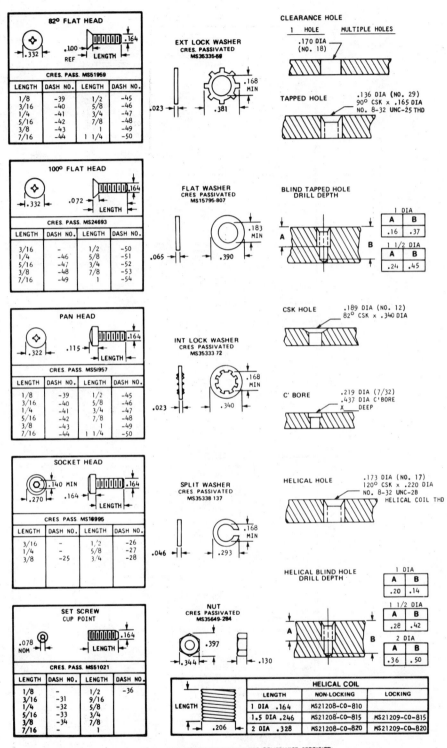

82° FLAT HEAD

.332 | .100 REF | LENGTH | .164

CRES. PASS. MS51969

LENGTH	DASH NO.	LENGTH	DASH NO.
1/8	-39	1/2	-45
3/16	-40	5/8	-46
1/4	-41	3/4	-47
5/16	-42	7/8	-48
3/8	-43	1	-49
7/16	-44	1 1/4	-50

100° FLAT HEAD

.332 | .072 | LENGTH | .164

CRES. PASS. MS24693

LENGTH	DASH NO.	LENGTH	DASH NO.
3/16	-	1/2	-50
1/4	-46	5/8	-51
5/16	-47	3/4	-52
3/8	-48	7/8	-53
7/16	-49	1	-54

PAN HEAD

.322 | .115 | LENGTH | .164

CRES. PASS. MS51957

LENGTH	DASH NO.	LENGTH	DASH NO.
1/8	-39	1/2	-45
3/16	-40	5/8	-46
1/4	-41	3/4	-47
5/16	-42	7/8	-48
3/8	-43	1	-49
7/16	-44	1 1/4	-50

SOCKET HEAD

.270 | .140 MIN | .164 | LENGTH | .164

CRES. PASS. MS16995

LENGTH	DASH NO.	LENGTH	DASH NO.
3/16	-	1/2	-26
1/4	-	5/8	-27
3/8	-25	3/4	-28

SET SCREW
CUP POINT

.078 NOM | LENGTH | .164

CRES. PASS. MS51021

LENGTH	DASH NO.	LENGTH	DASH NO.
1/8	-	1/2	-36
3/16	-31	9/16	
1/4	-32	5/8	
5/16	-33	3/4	
3/8	-34	7/8	
7/16	-	1	

EXT LOCK WASHER
CRES. PASSIVATED
MS35335-66

.023 | .381 | .168 MIN

FLAT WASHER
CRES PASSIVATED
MS15795-807

.065 | .390 | .183 MIN

INT LOCK WASHER
CRES PASSIVATED
MS35333 72

.023 | .340 | .168 MIN

SPLIT WASHER
CRES PASSIVATED
MS35338 137

.046 | .293 | .168 MIN

NUT
CRES PASSIVATED
MS35649-284

.344 | .397 | .130

CLEARANCE HOLE

1 HOLE   MULTIPLE HOLES

.170 DIA
(NO. 18)

TAPPED HOLE

.136 DIA (NO. 29)
90° CSK x .165 DIA
NO. 8-32 UNC-25 THD

BLIND TAPPED HOLE
DRILL DEPTH

A | B

	1 DIA	
	A	B
	.16	.37

	1 1/2 DIA	
	A	B
	.24	.45

CSK HOLE

.189 DIA (NO. 12)
82° CSK x .340 DIA

C' BORE

.219 DIA (7/32)
.437 DIA C'BORE
x DEEP

HELICAL HOLE

.173 DIA (NO. 17)
120° CSK x .220 DIA
NO. 8-32 UNC-2B
HELICAL COIL THD

HELICAL BLIND HOLE
DRILL DEPTH

A | B

	1 DIA	
	A	B
	.20	.14

	1 1/2 DIA	
	A	B
	.28	.42

	2 DIA	
	A	B
	.36	.50

HELICAL COIL

LENGTH		NON-LOCKING	LOCKING
1 DIA	.164	MS21208-CO-810	
1.5 DIA	.246	MS21208-CO-815	MS21209-CO-815
2 DIA	.328	MS21208-CO-820	MS21209-CO-820

LENGTH | .206

ALL DIMENSIONS ARE MAXIMUM UNLESS OTHERWISE SPECIFIED

10·32

ALL DIMENSIONS ARE MAXIMUM UNLESS OTHERWISE SPECIFIED

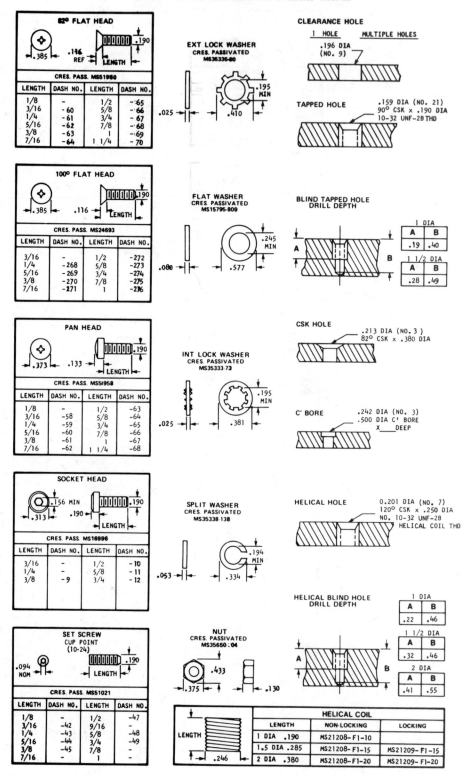

82° FLAT HEAD

.385 | .116 REF | .190 | LENGTH

CRES. PASS. MS51960

LENGTH	DASH NO.	LENGTH	DASH NO.
1/8	-	1/2	-65
3/16	-60	5/8	-66
1/4	-61	3/4	-67
5/16	-62	7/8	-68
3/8	-63	1	-69
7/16	-64	1 1/4	-70

100° FLAT HEAD

.385 | .116 | .190 | LENGTH

CRES. PASS. MS24693

LENGTH	DASH NO.	LENGTH	DASH NO.
3/16	-	1/2	-272
1/4	-268	5/8	-273
5/16	-269	3/4	-274
3/8	-270	7/8	-275
7/16	-271	1	-276

PAN HEAD

.373 | .133 | .190 | LENGTH

CRES. PASS. MS51958

LENGTH	DASH NO.	LENGTH	DASH NO.
1/8	-	1/2	-63
3/16	-58	5/8	-64
1/4	-59	3/4	-65
5/16	-60	7/8	-66
3/8	-61	1	-67
7/16	-62	1 1/4	-68

SOCKET HEAD

.313 | .156 MIN | .190 | .190 | LENGTH

CRES. PASS. MS16996

LENGTH	DASH NO.	LENGTH	DASH NO.
3/16	-	1/2	-10
1/4	-	5/8	-11
3/8	-9	3/4	-12

SET SCREW
CUP POINT
(10-24)

.094 NOM | .190 | LENGTH

CRES. PASS. MS51021

LENGTH	DASH NO.	LENGTH	DASH NO.
1/8	-	1/2	-47
3/16	-42	9/16	-
1/4	-43	5/8	-48
5/16	-44	3/4	-49
3/8	-45	7/8	-
7/16	-	1	-

EXT LOCK WASHER
CRES. PASSIVATED
MS35335-80

.025 | .410 | .195 MIN

FLAT WASHER
CRES. PASSIVATED
MS15795-809

.080 | .577 | .245 MIN

INT LOCK WASHER
CRES. PASSIVATED
MS35333-73

.025 | .381 | .195 MIN

SPLIT WASHER
CRES. PASSIVATED
MS35338-138

.053 | .334 | .194 MIN

NUT
CRES. PASSIVATED
MS35650-04

.375 | .433 | .130

CLEARANCE HOLE

1 HOLE   MULTIPLE HOLES

.196 DIA (NO. 9)

TAPPED HOLE

.159 DIA (NO. 21)
90° CSK x .190 DIA
10-32 UNF-2B THD

BLIND TAPPED HOLE
DRILL DEPTH

1 DIA	
A	B
.19	.40

1 1/2 DIA	
A	B
.28	.49

CSK HOLE

.213 DIA (NO. 3)
82° CSK x .380 DIA

C' BORE

.242 DIA (NO. 3)
.500 DIA C' BORE
X ___ DEEP

HELICAL HOLE

0.201 DIA (NO. 7)
120° CSK x .250 DIA
NO. 10-32 UNF-2B
HELICAL COIL THD

HELICAL BLIND HOLE
DRILL DEPTH

1 DIA	
A	B
.22	.46

1 1/2 DIA	
A	B
.32	.46

2 DIA	
A	B
.41	.55

HELICAL COIL

LENGTH | .246

LENGTH	NON-LOCKING	LOCKING
1 DIA .190	MS21208-F1-10	
1.5 DIA .285	MS21208-F1-15	MS21209-F1-15
2 DIA .380	MS21208-F1-20	MS21209-F1-20

1/4·28

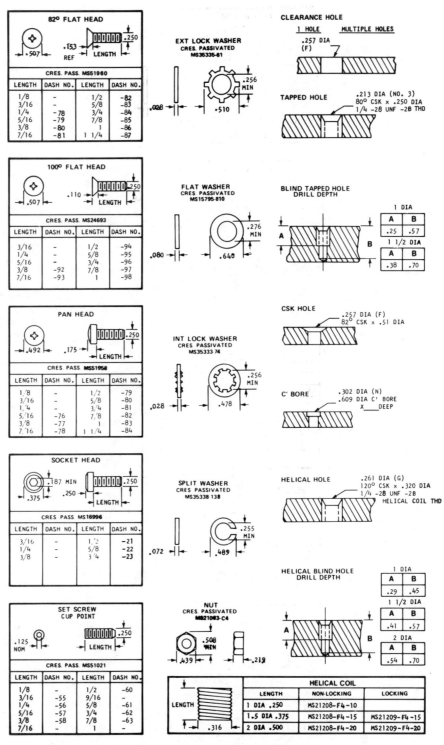

82° FLAT HEAD

.507 → | .153 REF | ← LENGTH → | .250

CRES. PASS. MS51960

LENGTH	DASH NO.	LENGTH	DASH NO.
1/8	–	1/2	-82
3/16	–	5/8	-83
1/4	-78	3/4	-84
5/16	-79	7/8	-85
3/8	-80	1	-86
7/16	-81	1 1/4	-87

100° FLAT HEAD

.507 → | .110 | ← LENGTH → | .250

CRES. PASS. MS24693

LENGTH	DASH NO.	LENGTH	DASH NO.
3/16	–	1/2	-94
1/4	–	5/8	-95
5/16	–	3/4	-96
3/8	-92	7/8	-97
7/16	-93	1	-98

PAN HEAD

.492 → | .175 | ← LENGTH → | .250

CRES. PASS. MS51958

LENGTH	DASH NO.	LENGTH	DASH NO.
1/8	–	1/2	-79
3/16	–	5/8	-80
1/4	–	3/4	-81
5/16	-76	7/8	-82
3/8	-77	1	-83
7/16	-78	1 1/4	-84

SOCKET HEAD

.375 → | .187 MIN | .250 | ← LENGTH → | .250

CRES. PASS. MS16996

LENGTH	DASH NO.	LENGTH	DASH NO.
3/16	–	1/2	-21
1/4	–	5/8	-22
3/8	–	3/4	-23

SET SCREW CUP POINT

.125 NOM → | ← LENGTH → | .250

CRES. PASS. MS51021

LENGTH	DASH NO.	LENGTH	DASH NO.
1/8	–	1/2	-60
3/16	-55	9/16	–
1/4	-56	5/8	-61
5/16	-57	3/4	-62
3/8	-58	7/8	-63
7/16	–	1	–

EXT LOCK WASHER
CRES. PASSIVATED
MS35335-81

.028 → | .256 MIN | .510

FLAT WASHER
CRES PASSIVATED
MS15795-810

.080 → | .276 MIN | .640

INT LOCK WASHER
CRES. PASSIVATED
MS35333-74

.028 → | .256 MIN | .478

SPLIT WASHER
CRES PASSIVATED
MS35338-138

.072 → | .255 MIN | .489

NUT
CRES. PASSIVATED
MS21083-C4

.439 → | .508 MIN | ← .219

CLEARANCE HOLE

| 1 HOLE | MULTIPLE HOLES |

.257 DIA (F)

TAPPED HOLE

.213 DIA (NO. 3)
80° CSK x .250 DIA
1/4 -28 UNF -2B THD

BLIND TAPPED HOLE DRILL DEPTH

1 DIA	
A	B
.25	.57

1 1/2 DIA	
A	B
.38	.70

CSK HOLE

.257 DIA (F)
82° CSK x .51 DIA

C' BORE

.302 DIA (N)
.609 DIA C' BORE
X___ DEEP

HELICAL HOLE

.261 DIA (G)
120° CSK x .320 DIA
1/4 -28 UNF -2B
HELICAL COIL THD

HELICAL BLIND HOLE DRILL DEPTH

1 DIA	
A	B
.29	.45

1 1/2 DIA	
A	B
.41	.57

2 DIA	
A	B
.54	.70

HELICAL COIL

LENGTH		NON-LOCKING	LOCKING
1 DIA .250		MS21208-F4-10	
1.5 DIA .375		MS21208-F4-15	MS21209-F4-15
2 DIA .500		MS21208-F4-20	MS21209-F4-20

LENGTH | .316

ALL DIMENSIONS ARE MAXIMUM UNLESS OTHERWISE SPECIFIED

INDEX